LASHKAR-I-TAIBA

Future of Islamist Terrorism in India

Attention Authors

Manas Publications is fighting a war to tell the world that India can win the battle not only by the bullet but also by pen. We are converting fighters into writers. There is no dearth of intellectuals in our country, however, their knowledge is confined to them only. No sincere effort has been made by any other publisher to channelise their knowledge, which is why the talent of every intellectual remains latent. An author always presents the raw material in the shape of a manuscript and it is the job of the publisher to convert it to a finished product. Manas has been continually motivating intellectuals and publishing their manuscripts for more than two decades and would like to publish your manuscript too. If you or your colleagues have a manuscript ready for publication or are working on it, contact us with a detailed synopsis and list of contents. Manas can also suggest you a suitable title for writing related to your area of expertise. Manas is known for its publishing quality. We take utmost care in publishing and also give wide publicity to the book and its author through our national and international distribution network.

LASHKAR-I-TAIBA

Future of Islamist Terrorism in India

US Army War College

Manas Publications
(We Convert Fighters into Writers)
New Delhi-110002 (INDIA)

MANAS PUBLICATIONS
(Publishers, Library Suppliers, Importers & Exporters)
4402/5-A, Ansari Road (Opp. HDFC Bank)
Darya Ganj, New Delhi-110 002 (INDIA)
Off. © 23260783, 23265523, Res. © 23842660
Fax: 011-23272766
E-mail: manaspublications@gmail.com
manaspublications@vsnl.com
Website: www.manaspublications.in

ISBN 978-81-7049-390-7
Rs. 495

Typeset at
Manas Publications

Printed in India at
RK Offset Process, Delhi
and published by Mrs Suman Lata for
Manas Publications, 4402/5-A, Ansari Road
(Opp. HDFC Bank),
Darya Ganj, New Delhi-110 002 (INDIA)

CONTENTS

SUMMARY

This work provides a discussion of the foundation of Lashkar-i-Taiba (LeT) and the development of its *modus operandi*, and it engages in an investigation of LeT activities in India, Pakistan, mainly the Kashmir region. Further, LeT fundraising methods are touched upon and LeT relationships with regional state and nonstate actors such as Pakistan's Inter-Services Intelligence (ISI) and Dawood Ibrahim's D-Company are analyzed. Also, the impact that these developments have on domestic Islamist terrorism in India are addressed. This work argues that although LeT has been a vital component of Islamabad's regional strategy in the past, the organization has grown beyond the control of its former patron, is largely self-sufficient, operating independently of the political process, and has expanded its agenda well beyond Kashmir. These developments challenge the long-held notion that irregulars can be sustainably used to achieve limited objectives in an asymmetric conflict and should serve as a clear warning to other state sponsors of terrorism. However, contrary to many analyses, LeT is not likely to sacrifice its independence and come under al- Qaeda's umbrella. Rather, LeT will continue to evolve into a distinctive, South Asia-centric terrorist actor in its own right while still receiving aid from fringe elements in Pakistan's security and intelligence apparatus and elsewhere. This will not only allow LeT to continue to plan future Mumbai-style terrorist attacks in India from safe havens in Pakistan, but will also allow LeT to guide and assist the predominantly indigenous Indian Mujahideen.

HISTORICAL OVERVIEW

Markaz-Dawa-ul-Irshad (Center for Preaching, also referred to as MDI) was founded in 1987 to assist the Afghan resistance against the Soviet Union and to purge Islam in Pakistan of what it viewed as the corrupting influence of Hinduism. Pakistan's Inter-Service Intelligence (ISI) and the US Central Intelligence Agency (CIA) utilized the Markaz during the Soviet invasion, but MDI was abandoned by the CIA after the Soviet withdrawal. However, ISI continued to use the organization to carry out attacks not only in Kashmir, but throughout India.[1] The founder of MDI was Hafiz Saeed, a professor of Islamic Studies at an engineering university in Pakistani Punjab. MDI is associated with the Wahhabi Ahl-e-Hadith orthodox school of thought that even forbids television and pictures. The religious philosophy of the Markaz is Sunni and intensely puritanical, and MDI publishes an Urdu magazine, *Al Dawa*, that has a reported circulation of around 80,000.[2]

The Markaz previously had close ties with Saudi Arabia, although differences emerged over MDI's relationship with Osama bin Laden and Riyadh's decision to allow US and other

Western troops to be stationed on Saudi soil. Osama bin Laden is reported to have contributed Pakistani rupees (Rs.) 10 million to the construction of a mosque at MDI's headquarters in Muridke, Pakistan, and is also believed to have built a guesthouse that he himself has stayed in. Further, it has been alleged that bin Laden used to attend the annual gatherings of the Markaz at Muridke but now only addresses them over conference phone from his hideouts in the former Sudan and the Afghanistan-Pakistan border area.[3]

Lashkar-i-Taiba (LeT) was formed slightly after the establishment of its parent organization, MDI, in the late 1980s.[4] LeT's militant activities began in the provinces of eastern Afghanistan in 1987-88 and focused primarily on engaging Soviet forces although LeT's role was minimal. Nonetheless, ISI felt that LeT had promising potential and began to take steps to shift LeT's focus to Kashmir.[5] By 1994, LeT was the militant wing of MDI, and unlike other irregular outfits that operated in Kashmir, the majority of LeT's fighters were non-Kashmiri mercenaries and based in Pakistan. In its early stages, LeT rejected offers of alliance with other indigenous Kashmiri groups in preference to operating independently and was largely ignored by other groups. However, LeT came to be respected after it began to engage in daring *fidayeen*[6] attacks against Indian security forces.[7] LeT also gained notoriety for its involvement in attacking Indian troops in synchronization with regular Pakistani forces during the 1999 Kargil conflict by occupying mountain top positions in upper Drass and Batalik.[8]

Muridke still serves as LeT's headquarters and is largely financed by Middle Eastern and Pakistani donors. This joint complex now consists of a madrassa, hospital, market, residences for scholars and faculty members, a fish farm, and agricultural tracts. In addition, some claim that LeT operates around 16 Islamic institutions, 135 secondary schools, an ambulance service, blood banks, and several seminaries across Pakistan.[9] LeT also runs a training camp in Bahawalpur (and in Punjab, a home also to Jaish-e-Mohammed) that has produced fighters who have engaged in terrorist acts throughout India.[10]

In October 2001, the United States declared LeT a terrorist organization and froze its assets that fell under US jurisdiction. Pakistan eventually followed suit and seized the group's assets in January 2002.[11] LeT was also banned by Pakistan's President Musharraf that same year, largely due to its alleged involvement in the September 11, 2001 (9/11) attacks, although LeT's involvement in the attack on the Indian Parliament in late 2001 was more likely the motivator.[12] Prior to this ban, LeT was permitted to operate openly in Pakistan, and nearly all shops in the main bazaar of every Pakistani town or city had a Lashkar donation box to assist in funding LeT's operations in Kashmir. LeT/ MDI head Hafiz Saeed was also briefly detained in 2002 but was set free after the Lahore High Court ruled that he was being unlawfully held. Upon his release, Saeed declared that it was the duty of every Muslim to wage jihad in Kashmir.[13]

Following this change in Musharraf's strategy, breakaway members of LeT began to attack the Pakistani political establishment and joined other militant groups under a loose anti-US banner. As a result of the ban by Musharraf, LeT is believed to have changed its name to Jama'at ud Dawa (which still functions as a charity across Pakistan) and continued its activities relatively unabated.[14] As such, the organization is still commonly referred to as LeT despite its official name change, and many question whether or not the current Zardari regime has the necessary support within the military establishment to fulfill its promises to crack down on the group. Some go so far to as to assert that Pakistan-based extremist activities will continue despite peace negotiations between Pakistan and India at the state level, thus seeming to suggest that Pakistan has created a monster that it can no longer control.[15] Many agree with this assessment and claim that Pakistan no longer exerts complete control over LeT and that there have been reports that LeT has a sizeable stockpile of weapons inside Jammu and Kashmir that will allow it to continue the insurgency for an appreciable period of tirne.[16]

LeT has fractionalized somewhat as a result of defections over Pakistan's policy of easing tensions with India. These elements feel that Saeed aligned his positions too closely to those of Musharraf and the current government as opposed to continuing to try to force India out of Kashmir.[17] The most notable defection was that of Maulana Zafar Iqbal, a former high-ranking LeT member who left the organization to form Khairun Naas (People's Welfare). Nonetheless, it is noteworthy that Khairun Naas has not emerged as a militant group thus far, and several prominent analysts believe the split was mainly the result of accusations of nepotism against Saeed.[18] This split caused serious tensions within LeT, but most analysts feel that this has not significantly weakened the group's operational capacities.[19] LeT has also experienced friction with other militant groups operating in Kashmir, such as Hizbul Mujahideen, thus causing some to believe that ISI has had to restructure the Pakistan-based United Jihad Council (UJC), a body that oversees many of the activities of the insurgent groups operating in Kashmir.[20] Although defections from LeT may initially appear to be positive, these developments could prove to have negative consequences. As has been demonstrated by other pan-Islamist groups, such as Indonesia-based Jemaah Islamiyah (JI), defectors often form more violent splinter groups that not only cause more damage, but also provide security personnel and policymakers with a whole new list of variables to account for, thus making the dismantling (or at least containment and/or deterrence) of a group such as LeT all the more complicated.

GOALS

Saeed has stated that Kashmir is the "gateway to capture India" and that LeT would begin to push for independence of majority-Muslim areas in India such as Gujurat and Hyderabad (Andhra Pradesh).[21] Further, some claim that LeT aims not only to eject India from Kashmir, but also seeks to re-establish Islamic rule over the entire Indian Union.[22] However, others disagree and assert that despite the fact that LeT has advocated extending its "jihad" from J&K to the rest of India, its goal is to establish two independent homelands for Muslims in southern and northern India.[23] Nonetheless, LeT has forged relationships with militant movements (though the strength of these ties is the source of much debate) in Afghanistan, Bosnia, the Palestinian territories, and Kashmir in order to pool resources, share experience, and to improve the effectiveness of their operations.[24] However, these partnerships are a reflection of shared tactical interests rather than a by-product of a larger strategic alignment. Although its infrastructure spans the globe, LeT prioritizes the South Asian theater regarding its operations and propaganda efforts. Much of this cooperation is simply information exchange and the sharing of best practices and tactics. Affiliation with iconic struggles such as the Palestinian issue also helps to boost legitimacy amongst potential as well as currentdonors and aids recruitment efforts within Pakistan.

Many analysts point to the joint attack by LeT and Jaish-e-Mohammed (JeM) on the Indian Parliament in December 2001 that brought India and Pakistan to the brink of war as proof positive that there were not massive differences between the Kashmir-centered terrorist groups in terms of their strategic thinking and use of tactics, and that many of the differentiations between the groups were artificial. However, such analyses fail to realize that LeT does not view itself as one among equals but rather as the premier terrorist group in South Asia. Though it recognizes and likely respects the capabilities of JeM and others, the joint attack on Parliament was the result of a desire by LeT (and possibly JeM) to share risk in what was likely somewhat of an experiment in the use of *fidayeen* attacks in a major urban environment and possibly a precursor for the November 2008 Mumbai attacks. Unlike suicide bombing, even though the death of a *fidayeen* attacker is likely, it is not guaranteed and interrogations of too many LeT cadre could severely damage the group's operational security and its networks in India. The lesson to take away from this episode is that while LeT will partner with like-minded groups to obtain short-term benefits and to enhance its organizational learning, LeT still charts its own path and views such partnerships as a component of its strategy to become the most effective terrorist organization in the Subcontinent.

Although there is considerable disagreement regarding LeT's motives aside from ridding Kashmir of Indian rule, two statements from Saeed in 1996 and 1997 provide substantial insight. Speaking to journalists, Saeed said:

> The jihad in Kashmir would soon spread to entire India. Our Mujahideen would create three Pakistans in India.
>
> We feel that Kashmir should be liberated at the earliest. Thereafter, Indian Muslims should be aroused to rise in revolt against the Indian Union so that India gets disintegrated.[25]

These direct quotes clearly illustrate that even though LeT's initial focus was on Kashmir, the organization has developed a more radical regional agenda and is willing to use the Kashmir conflict as a beacon to carry out attacks throughout India. Further, evidence suggests that LeT seeks to establish an Islamic Caliphate of all Muslim-majority states surrounding Pakistan, is believed to have become involved in Chechnya and other parts of Central Asia, and has trained other Pan-Islamist militant groups such as

JI in Pakistan-held Kashmir and Afghanistan.[26] In addition to India, Saeed considers Israel and the United States as LeT's primary enemies.[27] The controversial B. Raman even alleges that on behalf of the bin Laden-founded International Islamic Front for Jihad Against the Crusaders and the Jewish People (IIF), LeT issued a *fatwa* claiming that it was the duty of all Muslims to kill the Pope.[28] It is also noteworthy that LeT has links to al-Qaeda, as was demonstrated by the March 2002 arrest of senior al- Qaeda lieutenant Abu Zubaydah in a LeT safe house in Faisalabad, Pakistan. This arrest gave rise to the belief that LeT assists in the movements of al-Qaeda fighters within Pakistan.[29] All of this demonstrates that Pakistan's initial belief that it could use proxies to wage an asymmetric conflict with limited objectives against an adversary (India) was clearly misguided. More than 2 decades later, as opposed to remaining deeply committed to Pakistan and even more obedient to its limited objectives, as Islamabad undoubtedly intended, LeT now threatens Pakistan's own security with its activities throughout South Asia and runs counter to Pakistan's own declared policies thus jeopardizing its already-tenuous relationship with India as well as the United States, United Kingdom (UK), other Western powers, and even its long-time ally, China. In regards to the latter, Beijing interprets the rising unrest in its Muslim-majority Xinjiang province as a result of happenings in South and Central Asia.

LeT's recent involvement in the November 2008 attacks in Mumbai possibly represents a considerable shift in the organization's strategic thought. Although some of the gunmen were undoubtedly Pakistani, sustained attacks on such symbolic targets could not have occurred without Indian assets. Further, although the majority of victims were Indians, the militants also deliberately targeted foreigners, namely British and American citizens as well as Israelis. These practices are new to LeT and suggest an increasing ideological overlap with more prominent transnational terrorist groups such as al-Qaeda. The timing of the attacks also cannot be ignored as they occurred during the first sustained Pakistani offensive against al-Qaeda and both the Afghan and Pakistani Taliban in the tribal areas. It can be reasonably argued that the primary intention of this attack was to reignite hostilities between India and Pakistan, thus forcing Pakistan to redeploy a large portion of its troops from the tribal areas to its eastern border with India. As such, the possibility of tactical cooperation between LeT and other regional antagonists, such as Afghan/Pakistani Taliban as well as al-Qaeda, cannot be ruled out.

Chapter - I

LeT IN KASHMIR

Under the banner of LeT, foreign mercenaries were first introduced into Kashmir in 1993 and were dispersed within the mountainous regions. In this same year, the Islami Inqalbi Mahaz camp in Poonch District was established near the Line of Control (LOC) with the help of ISI and Pakistani military officers, and by 1994 LeT was ready to undertake major operations throughout the Kashmir Valley. At first, local militant groups were wary of LeT as its fighters were mostly foreign mercenaries and much more fundamentalist than the locals.[30] Although this suspicion has subsided somewhat, it has not entirely evaporated as some indigenous groups question whether a mercenary dominated LeT represents the interests of the Kashmiri people or Islamabad's foreign policy objectives.

LeT's first mission was in October 1994 when a group of 50-60 militants ambushed an Indian army convoy and abducted and eventually executed five army personnel, including two officers. Since 1994, LeT has engaged in numerous attacks on not only Indian security forces in Kashmir, but also on Muslim and non-Muslim civilians. Further, *fidayeen* attacks such as the December 27, 1999, mission on the Indian Special Operations Group (SOG) headquarters have become a LeT trademark.[31]

Even though LeT was in possession of considerable resources in the early 1990s, its successful establishment in Kashmir would not have been possible without ISI assistance. The construction of Islami Inqalbi Mahaz near the heavily fortified LOC would have required transport capabilities, smuggling expertise, and local contacts, all of which would have required a significant logistics capacity, something that LeT unlikely had in its possession. Stanley Bedlington, a former CIA official, supports this view and claims that ISI was intricately involved in LeT's initial development.[32]

Although ISI was heavily involved in the early years of LeT, LeT clearly does not view itself as accountable to Pakistan any longer. Its involvement in the November 2008 Mumbai attack is testimony to this as it occurred at a very inopportune moment for Pakistan. At present, Pakistan is suffering from an economic crisis, surging inflation, a poorly-performing stock market, and considerable internal instability as a result of a myriad of militant groups. Rising tensions with India and the possibility of war would exacerbate all of these difficulties and strengthen the position of extremist groups in the country. None of this is in Pakistan's interest, and if LeT was overly concerned about maintaining favor with Pakistan its leadership would not engage in such a reckless operation.

RECRUITMENT

LeT recruits and trains many more militants than it actually needs to fight in Kashmir at a given time, thus reducing its vulnerability to a massive strike and ensuring that the organization maintains an ample supply of reserves.[33] LeT is also believed to be in possession of thousands of weapons including a substantial number of Chinese hand grenades and an unknown number of Chinese pistols.[34] Most of LeT's recruits come from madrassas in Pakistan, and even a few within India.[35] Although some may find it hard to believe that LeT actually recruits Indian nationals to carry out attacks against their own country, the April 2, 2007, arrest of an ISI agent in Hyderabad is a clear demonstration that LeT does not view the Indian Union as inaccessible. The agent was detained for recruiting youth on behalf of LeT and JeM to engage in militant activity in Hyderabad and Gujarat.[36]

The Student Islamic Movement of India (SIMI) was suspected of involvement in the July 2006 Mumbai train bombings (commonly referred to as the 7/11 bombings). It is alleged that they worked alongside of Pakistan-based LeT operatives and assisted them in illegally entering India. This home-grown militant group has gained power and influence over recent years and does not show signs of weakening. LeT experienced an increase in the recruiting of SIMI activists following the anti-Muslim riots in Bombay (Bombay was renamed Mumbai in 1995) in the 1990s and in Gujarat in 2002.[37] However, Marwah, of the Institute for Defence Studies and Analyses (IDSA), India's key strategic think tank, believes that even though some Indian Muslims have begun to take a more anti-India stance, they have done so to increase pressure on New Delhi to give them more influence in the political system, but not necessarily because of Islamic extremist tendencies.[38] Marwah's point is debatable. The fact that LeT now has operatives based in New Delhi, Mumbai, and other major Indian cities and was able to recruit Indian citizens to carry out attacks within India demonstrates that there exists some degree of sympathy towards their radical ideology, although the exact numbers are unknown. Evidence has recently come to light that alleges that LeT has recruited thousands of mostly-Punjabi men ages 18 to 25 for operations in Iraq and that LeT hopes to send suicide bombers overland to Iraq through the porous Pakistan-Iran border.[39] If accurate, this development is a clear demonstration of the increasing independence that LeT is exhibiting in its decision making as it seeks to expand its scope of operations and possibly extend its influence outside the subcontinent. Further, by dispatching fighters to Middle Eastern conflict zones such as Iraq, LeT would be attempting to forge broader partnerships with likeminded militant groups, a move that would enhance LeT's operational capabilities and diversify its financial support base, thus further lessening its dependence on Islamabad and guaranteeing its continued existence in the medium term. However, it is of note that suicide bombings have not yet been used by LeT. Also, expect LeT to continue to prioritize South Asia while viewing the Middle East as a potential source of expert knowledge and funds.

LeT's India-centric recruitment efforts were not likely foreseen by many in Pakistan aside from the extremist elements within the government that were involved in the gradual evolution of the group. The initial decision to nurture and gradually introduce LeT into Kashmir was based on the premise that it would remain there at Islamabad's behest to carry out limited objectives vis-a-vis India but would not make any ill-advised moves that would escalate tensions to an unacceptable level. For nearly 2 decades, this analysis appeared to hold true until several international events and at least an official policy reversal by Pakistan regarding its support for irregulars prompted a dramatic revision in LeT's strategic thinking. This revision caused it to morph from a subservient proxy strictly following directives, while being careful not to harm Pakistani interests, to a group that is now overtly hostile to Islamabad and makes most of its own decisions. This lesson should not be lost in several capitals, namely Damascus and Tehran, and it must be recognized that when it comes to state sponsorship of terrorism or insurgency, no two actors have identical interests; and long-established ties do not mean that they are permanent or not subject to a review or even outright reversal by either party. However, by this time the nonstate actor has often developed an intimate knowledge of the society, economy, and governance structure of its former patron, thus allowing it to target the patron with increased lethality and effectiveness.

ACTIVITIES AND OPERATING STRUCTURE OF LeT

LeT is one of the most dangerous groups operating in Kashmir and throughout India. Even though most of its ranks are filled with fighters from Pakistan, LeT has militants from places such as the Central Asian Republics and a variety of other nations.[40] Its membership is not believed to be much more than 500 core members, thus demonstrating its efficiency in moving fighters, planning and executing attacks, and utilizing scarce human resources.[41] In addition to *fidayeen* attacks, LeT engages in guerrilla-style hit and run tactics that have targeted Indian civilians, politicians, and security forces as well as police stations, hotels, airports, border outposts, and public transportation.[42]

LeT cadre is divided into districts and at the field level, LeT is organized in a militaristic fashion with a chief commander, provisional commander, district commander, battalion commander, and so on. The group also has a policymaking body that comprises an amir (chief), naib amir (deputy chief), and various other strategists that are organized in a hierarchal fashion. LeT has training camps and recruitment offices throughout Pakistan and Pakistan-held Kashmir in places such as Muzaffarabad, Lahore, Peshawar, Islamabad, Rawalpindi, Multan, Quetta, Gujranwala, Sialkot, and Gilgit.[43] However, LeT's largest Pakistan based camp is believed to be in Muzaffarabad, and its most active training centers are believed to be in Pakistan-held Kashmir.[44] Further, in 2005 Wilson John claimed that within Pakistan-held Kashmir, LeT runs 24 forward operating camps along the LOC.[45] LeT has also established charitable organizations that reward the families of "martyrs" whose sons have died in Kashmir.[46]

Some believe that LeT has an arms training center in Kunar province in Afghanistan that can train up to 600 militants at one time.[47] However, others dispute this on the grounds that US Special Forces have recently established a base in the province, that the area is extremely hostile to outsiders, and that LeT would not be welcome due to the fact that it receives funds from Wahhabis in Saudi Arabia. As such, they claim that if LeT even has camps in the area, they are mobile ones capable of training a handful of fighters at a time before having to move to another location. In addition, they believe that any alleged LeT fighters in Afghanistan are breakaway members as LeT remains focused on Kashmir and the Indian Union.[48]

Nonetheless, there have also been allegations that, according to Afghan media, LeT has been recruiting Afghan refugees to take up arms against Afghan President Karzai's government in Kabul and has begun to collect donations in Jalozai on behalf of the Taliban.[49] Further, LeT is reported to be active in Nuristan, an isolated, dangerous, and warlord-ruled area of northeastern Afghanistan and has fighters stationed there. Due to high levels of violence and random attacks, Nuristan has a very small amount of foreigners, thus allowing warlords, militants, and criminals alike to travel and operate freely. The inter-tribal violence combined with a general sense of lawlessness even deters state officials, and has allowed LeT to gain a strong foothold in the region and to develop vested interests in ensuring that the current situation in Nuristan prevails. Nuristan serves as a major supply line for insurgent groups operating in the region and is home to Gulbuddin Hekmatyar's at-times pro-Pakistan Hezb-i-Islami.[50] This overlap in operating areas between LeT and Hezb-i-Islami is problematic for Kashmir for a number of reasons. First, it provides both organizations with the opportunity for information exchange and joint training that would in turn enhance LeT's tactics in Kashmir as Hezb-i-Islami is a well-experienced, battle hardened group whose leader has been engaging foreign and domestic forces since the Soviet invasion. Second, it would allow LeT to expand its network base through Hekmatyar's extensive regional and global contacts. Lastly, there have been allegations in the past that Islamabad has used Hezb-i-Islami to stage attacks in Kashmir, and, if these accusations are true, the fighters likely came from Nuristan. If Nuristan-based groups cooperate with LeT to engage Indian security forces in Kashmir in the future, it could further complicate diplomacy between Islamabad and New Delhi as both would have to account for a third regional party (Afghanistan) whose leadership has been openly hostile to Pakistan.

In addition to operations in India, Pakistan, and Afghanistan, LeT is believed to have underground cells in the UK, France, Australia, the United States, and possibly Italy.[51] These overseas cells likely serve predominantly fundraising purposes and solicit the Pakistani diaspora and other sympathetic Muslim groups. However, given LeT's supposed involvement in the 2004 Madrid train bombings and its links with al-Qaeda, it would be naïve to assume that LeT is not willing to carry out attacks on Western soil. Further, the June 2004 arrest of LeT operative Danish Ahmed in Basra by British forces demonstrates that the group is at least seeking to become active in the Iraqi insurgency. At the time of his arrest, Ahmed claimed that over 2,000 fighters had committed to LeT-led operations against US troops in Iraq. LeT's Urdu weekly, *Gazwa* (Assault on the Unbelievers), often calls upon Pakistanis to fight in Iraq.[52]

LeT cells in the West will spell trouble for any Pakistani efforts to reign in the organization as the Pakistani diaspora, some of whom have become very financially successful overseas while still harboring extremist tendencies, could fill the void left by Islamabad by providing pounds, euros, and dollars through the vast Hawala system in the Gulf and South Asia. Any such move would serve to undercut the actions taken by the Pakistani government and would keep LeT afloat. In addition, as LeT has made inroads in several European nations, it will likely expand to other wealthy European nations with sizeable Muslim populations. Since any individual holding a valid visa or passport from an European Union (EU) nation is granted freedom of movement throughout the entire bloc. This allows LeT to take advantage of Europe's extensive and highly integrated financial and transportation infrastructure. Also, similarly to what has been seen in Europe regarding the Liberation Tigers of Tamil Eelam (LTTE), low awareness levels as well as a lack of research on LeT has assisted the group's efforts and has given it more operating space than what it would otherwise enjoy.

Chapter - 2

LeT IN INDIA

As LeT has been active in Kashmir and throughout India for an appreciable period of time, the group has been implicated in a long list of attacks. A comprehensive (but not exhaustive) list includes:

- LeT carried out Hindu massacres in January 1996, January 1997, June 1997, and April, June, and August 1998.[53]
- LeT was involved in the slaughter of at least 35 Sikh civilians in Chattisinghpura during President Clinton's March 2000 visit to the region.[54] One LeT militant, 18-year-old Suhail Malik, who was involved in the attacks, was quoted as saying: "The Koran teaches us not to kill innocents. (But) if Lashkar-e-Taiyba told us to kill these people (Sikhs), then it was the right thing to do. I have no regrets."[55]
- In 2000, LeT attempted to assassinate Shiv Sena head Bal Thakery, a Bombay-based hardline Hindu nationalist leader.[56]

- LeT attacked the Indian Army barracks at Red Fort in Delhi in 2000.[57]

  LeT's involvement in an armed raid on India's parliament in December 2001 nearly brought India and Pakistan into an all-out war.[58] India has accused ISI of providing the support to LeT that enabled them to carry out the attack.[59]

- In 2001, LeT claimed responsibility for an attack on Srinagar airport that killed five Indians and six militants, as well as an attack in the same city on a police station that killed eight officers and wounded several others .[60]
- LeT is accused of an attack on two Hindu temples in Jammu and Kashmir in 2002.[61]
- A May 14, 2002, LeT attack on an Indian Army base in Kaluchak, killing 36.[62]
- In September 2003, it was revealed that LeT was planning to bomb the U.S. embassy in Delhi.[63]
- LeT was blamed for the 2005 Diwali bombings in New Delhi that killed over 60 people. LeT denied involvement.[64]
- LeT allegedly carried out an attack on the Indian Institute of Science in Bangalore in December 2005 which resulted in one death.
- LeT was involved in an attack in Varanasi in March 2006.
- In June 2006, three LeT operatives were killed while attempting to infiltrate the headquarters of Rashtriya Swayamsevak Sangh (RSS), a right-wing nationalist group, in Nagpur, Maharashtra.
- LeT is accused by the Bombay (Mumbai) police of having carried out the July 11, 2006 (7/11) serial bombings that killed at least 200.[65] India also claims

that the preparations were made by ISI, executed by LeT operatives, and that SIMI was a participating party as well. India believes that all 11 LeT operatives were Pakistanis and entered India in small groups from Pakistan, Bangladesh, and Nepal.[66]

- LeT is believed to be involved in the bombs that exploded outside a mosque in Malegaon a few weeks after the 7/11 blasts.[67] However, recent investigations suggest that these actions may have been carried out by Hindu extremists.
- The CIA reported that LeT had been directed by a foreign organization to assassinate the Dalai Lama. As a result, security around the Tibetan leader-in-exile had to be tightened.[68]
- LeT has widely been accused of the November 2008 attacks in Mumbai.

These attacks demonstrate that LeT often does not differentiate between combatants and civilians and is willing to hit both hard and soft targets. Further, these actions illustrate that not only does LeT attack other religious groups, such as Hindus and Sikhs, but it also does not seem to have many reservations about placing Muslims in harm's way either. Many LeT operatives are young, fanatical, and have access to an underground infrastructure that allows them to function throughout the whole of India, not merely Kashmir. As such, it is unrealistic to suggest that the problem of Islamic militancy within India can be solved through sound law enforcement tactics alone. Any counterterrorism strategy has to be comprehensive and would have to address issues on both sides of the border such as poverty, unemployment, access to secular education, and sufficient oversight of madrassas. Further, sensitive topics such as domestic sympathy for anti-Indian Islamic groups must be analyzed objectively and necessary changes need to be implemented.

Several recent high-profile arrests and interrogations over the 7/11 bombings have shed light onto LeT's modes of operation within India: Pakistan-based LeT commander Azam Cheema (still at large) has been determined to have been responsible for transferring RDX ("rapidly detonating explosive"—a powerful noncommercial explosive) to India and using Pakistan based militants to assemble the bombs. Further, LeT Bombay head Faisal Shaikh was arrested for receiving arms training in Pakistan and organizing funding for the 7/11 attacks via the Hawala system, as well as for planting the bomb which exploded in the Jogeshwari railway station. In addition, Asif Khan Bashir Khan was taken into custody over his involvement in housing Pakistani militants that crossed over the Indo-Bangla border and for securing bomb making materiel and assisting in bomb making.[69] Trafficking Pakistani fighters into India through Bangladesh would have required cooperation with Pakistani intelligence and Bangladesh-based Harakat-ul-Jihad-i-Islami Bangladesh (HUJI-B), a group that has been largely cultivated by Pakistan but is now Bangladesh-centric, has close ties to Jamaat-e-Islami, and is involved in planning attacks on Indian interests and committing acts of economic sabotage such as the circulation of counterfeit currency in an attempt to undermine the strength of the Indian rupee, something which is actually not possible. Majid Mohammed Shafi, a Kolkata native, is accused of smuggling RDX and Pakistani militants across the Indian border with Bangladesh, thus demonstrating that LeT has a network within the Union that consists of Indian-born militants. Sajid Margub Ansari, an Indian SIMI activist who ran a mobile phone repair shop, was arrested for providing timer-related electric circuitry and other devices. Further, Ehteshaam Siddiqui, a fellow Bombay-based SIMI operative, was detained for harboring militants, conducting surveillance on local trains along with several other SIMI fighters, and assisting in the assembling of bombs.[70] These particular arrests are a testimony to the fact that in addition to having Indian natives at their disposal, LeT also liaises with Indian-based subversive groups such as the outlawed SIMI.[71]

Kamal Ansari, who hails from the Madhubani district in Uttar Pradesh, received arms training in Pakistan and was tasked with bringing in Pakistani militants via Nepal.[72] Once again, these operations would not be possible without Pakistani assistance, as these smuggling operations would have to be well planned and adequately resourced. Although the Indo-Nepal border has historically been porous, efforts would need to have been made for the militants to avoid detection. Provisions likely included fake travel documents, substantial sums of currency, "clean" phones, etc. It is noteworthy that Dawood Ibrahim's D-Company has a significant presence in Nepal, and that this particular nation served as an exit point for some of his operatives that absconded following their involvement in the 1993 Bombay Blasts. ISI is also active in Nepal, as was demonstrated by the August 1, 2007, arrest of Abdul Wahab, a Pakistani national and ISI agent who was detained in Kathmandu with US $252,000 of counterfeit Indian currency.[73] Although the extent of cooperation between ISI and D-Company is debatable, it is apparent that Ibrahim does not have an issue with pairing with ISI to launch attacks on his native country in areas where he feels Muslims are suffering at the hands of the Hindu majority. The fact that one of the 7/11 bombs was placed in Jogeshwari, an area that is notorious for sometimes,brutal communal violence, is a clear indication that the main motivation for the attacks was ideological. Although the 1993 attacks on Bombay were conducted mostly by D-Company and ISI operatives, the 7/11 bombings involved the relatively new LeT, a group that has formed a strategic alliance with Ibrahim and D-Company, a partnership that has developed largely as a result of Ibrahim's refuge in Pakistan. Ironically, Pakistan's fostering of ties between LeT and a transnational criminal syndicate has further lessened Islamabad's leverage and the likelihood that LeT will follow orders since it provides LeT with further opportunities to obtain and maintain financial independence.

On July 13, 2007, India's Anti-Terrorist Squad (ATS) of the Pune police arrested LeT operative Mohammed Bilal. Bilal had been living in Pune for 7 months while studying at a city college and working at a private firm.[74] The actions of Bilal highlight a harsh reality in that even though India has made some strides in strengthening border security and intelligence capacities, sleeper operatives such as Bilal are still able to infiltrate and violate Indian sovereignty. Further, despite the fact that the ATS treated this arrest as a major success, it is unclear whether they were successful in dismantling the cell that Bilal had undoubtedly established, or worked within, while a resident of Pune.

Another troubling development for New Delhi is the recent arrest of three LeT operatives in the Indian capital that originated from Manipur. The militants were in possession of two kilograms of RDX, two detonators, and a hand grenade, and were the first LeT operatives hailing from any Northeastern state with intent to attack New Delhi. Some believe that this demonstrates how vulnerable India's Northeastern regions are to terrorist groups.[75] Others add to these concerns, stating that with LeT support, Meitei Pangal (Manipuri Muslims) could grow in strength and even challenge already established anti-center Meitei insurgent groups, thus leading to further instability in the already-impoverished state.[76] There have also been reports that LeT, along with HUJI-B and Jama'atul Mujahideen Bangladesh (JMB), has made inroads in Assam, the Northeast's most populous and strategically important state. These groups are alleged to have forged partnerships with the United Liberation Front of Assam (ULFA) and have established several bases within Assam's Dhubri district, which runs along India's border with Bangladesh. The *modus operandi* of groups in the Northeast is to attack government forces, economic targets, and the petroleum sector, in addition to other soft targets such as market places.[77] These aims could be very problematic, given Assam's large oil and natural gas reserves that are much needed by a resource-hungry and expanding Indian economy. Instability in the Northeast also deprives India of a vital economic corridor to the markets of Southeast Asia and ensures that the region remains underdeveloped and plagued by instability.

Recent trends in arrests suggest that militant groups are beginning to target major Indian cities with LeT becoming the most dangerous and persistent. Further, LeT has begun to smuggle its fighters into India by sea as was highlighted by the March 10, 2007, arrests of LeT operatives in the Rajauri district of J&K. Subsequent interrogations revealed that eight of the militants had entered India via a boat that set off from Karachi. In addition, a January 3, 2007, Indian Intelligence Bureau report claims that a sizeable amount of LeT cadre are trained to handle large boats and in other navigational skills, to lay land mines and explosives, and in various types of surveillance methods with the aim of increasing LeT's ability to enter India through its coastal regions and/or island territories.[78] Some of these skills were used to enter Mumbai for the most recent attacks.

Many of the vessels that are used to violate India's sea borders and to move fighters into its territory are undoubtedly sourced from Karachi, a city well-known for its vast and unregulated ports that provide an ideal environment for organized criminal syndicates to operate and for elements in ISI to engage in some of their more nefarious activities. The potential role of D-Company in this relatively new LeT endeavour cannot be ignored. As was demonstrated by the 1993 Bombay Blasts, Ibrahim not only has control over much of the smuggling activity that occurs in Karachi, but also has the rare ability to engage in smuggling on the high seas. If D-Company was able to smuggle enough small arms and light weapons into Bombay to fight a small war during a time of heightened security following the anti-Muslim riots of 1992 and early 1993, the syndicate would not be hard pressed to smuggle a select group of militants on smaller, more inconspicuous ships, some of which may be nothing more than small fishing boats. ISI could not only utilize the expertise and local contacts of D-Company, but could also use the plausible deniability that Ibrahim's syndicate can provide to Islamabad since state involvement in organized criminal activity is notoriously difficult to prove. Further, the fact that this cooperation occurs between two nonstate actors that Pakistan does not claim to support makes the chances of independent verification even less likely.

FUNDING

LeT collects donations from the overseas Pakistani community in the Persian Gulf and the UK, Islamic nongovernmental organizations (NGOs), Pakistani/ Kashmiri businesspeople, and through its parent organization, Jamaat-ud-Dawa.[79] The militant group also counts on donations from sympathetic Saudis, Kuwaitis, and Islamist-leaning ISI leaders.[80] In addition, LeT maintains relations with extremist and/ or terrorist groups across the globe ranging from the Philippines to the Middle East and Chechnya by means of the Jamaat-ud-Dawa network. Although most of LeT's monetary assets were previously deposited in mainstream financial institutions, many of these deposits were withdrawn and invested in legitimate ventures such as commodity trading, real estate, and manufacturing in order to avoid seizures following Musharraf's crackdown on Pakistan-based militant groups.[81] This black money has likely been funneled through numerous intermediaries, and a substantial portion may have even left Pakistan via the underground Hawala system. Either resulting from a lack of political will or of enforcement capacity, Pakistan's measures to cut terrorist financing remain woefully inadequate.

The October 2005 earthquake provided LeT with an opportunity to once again openly raise funds in Pakistan by soliciting donations toward official construction work. Since the natural disaster, many LeT offices have been reopened, and its members have been given a primary role in construction projects.[82] The presence of militants in LeT camps in Pakistan-held Kashmir made it possible for them to engage in early rescue missions during the earthquake's aftermath; operations that they sought to use to cultivate a strong local support base.[83] Further, the arrest of Pakistan based LeT operative Ejaz Ahmad Bhat in Srinigar just 5 days after the earthquake suggests that LeT strategists sought to capitalize on the goodwill that was generated through relief operations and to recruit new younger members.[84] Also troubling are the assertions of Partlow and Khan that allege that the transfer of millions of pounds from the UK to a Pakistani charity that was engaging in earthquake relief assisted investigators in uncovering a plot to blow up two U.S.-bound airplanes. According to Pakistani officials, a large portion of the funds sent from Britain were siphoned off and used to prepare the attacks; and out of the US $10 million that was originally sent, much of which was likely sent to Jamaat-ud-Dawa, less than half was used in relief operations.[85]

The July 2006 arrest of Faizal Sheik by the ATS shed light onto LeT's underground fund-raising network within India as he is suspected of serving as the group's Bombay-based fundraiser who acquired funds from Pakistan and the Middle East via the Hawala system.[86] This occurrence is highly problematic for Indian security planners in that if strong cross-border links exist between Hawala dealers, the cutting of terrorist financing within India will prove very difficult. Hawala is an informal banking system that is built upon trust and seasoned relationships between actors and even if arrests are made, given the close personal ties within the network, interrogations often do not yield desired results. In some instances in South Asia, those involved in transnational

Hawala banking are even related. Further, the fact that this particular arrest was made in Mumbai, India's financial and organized crime epicenter, is significant. Although Sheik likely did channel funds from Pakistan and the Middle East to LeT, it would be reasonable to assume that he collected funds from within India as well. Mumbai is not a stranger to communal strife, and while many Indian Muslims reap the monetary benefits of India's (and especially Mumbai's) economic growth, a small but powerful minority will continue to have more money to donate towards what they perceive as a just cause. Also, D-Company thrives on both sides of the border, especially in Karachi and Mumbai, and is widely believed to have a monopoly over illegal Hawala transactions. Given this reality, along with D-Company's partnership with LeT and the syndicate's past experience in utilizing their Bombay network to provide funding and weaponry for the 1993 Bombay blasts, it is a fair assumption that Dawood Ibrahim and Faizal Sheik enjoyed at least a working relationship.

In addition to soliciting donations from charities, NGOs, and overseas Pakistanis, LeT has branched out and diversified its sources of funding, thus making its financial pipeline less vulnerable to a decapitating strike. Harvard's Jessica Stern claims that LeT has begun to raise funds on the internet and has acquired so much capital (mostly from Saudi Arabian Wahhabis) that it is actually planning to open its own bank. Some mid-level LeT commanders earn Rs.15,000 a month (seven times more than the average Pakistani), and some top leaders often earn more. One such leader provided Stern a glimpse of his mansion that was staffed by servants and filled with expensive furniture.[87] LeT is also funded by the same networks of legitimate commercial enterprises that covertly fund al-Qaeda, and although the exact amount of funding available to LeT is unknown, it has been reported that the organization was able to raise roughly US $4 million in the UK in 2001 alone.[88] LeT has even generated revenue through the selling of as many as 1.2 million hides of animals that were sacrificed during Eid, a Muslim festival.[89]

Aside from a few arrests/seizures and reports issued by various arms of the Indian government, there exists little research regarding LeT involvement in drug-trafficking for fund-raising purposes. However, given LeT's areas of operation, strategic and ideologically-based alliances, and the need to secure capital from a balanced range of sources, LeT is likely to be involved in the trade. Given the huge profit margins that narcotics trafficking can yield, it would allow LeT to act more independently as it would not have as many reservations about undertaking actions that may result in a loss of state funding or donations from other parties. It would also reduce LeT's chances of being held hostage to Islamabad's agenda. Kunnar and Nuristan serve as ideal exit points for the Afghan poppy trade as strong ethnic and linguistic links on both sides of the Afghan/Pak border greatly facilitate smuggling. Further, as the arm of Kabul does not reach Nuristan, traffickers can operate with impunity and not only funnel narcotics eastward towards Pakistan, India, and China, but also into Tajikistan and several other Central Asian nations, and from there into the lucrative markets in Russia and the West. As Afghanistan now supplies roughly [92] percent of the world's opium poppies, and as production is predicted to continue to rise, strong multidimensional regional networks have been established (or simply reestablished in some cases) to fully capitalize on this development. These networks, combined with massive profit potential, would prove too much for LeT to resist, especially after their official 2002 proscription.

The US Drug Enforcement Administration (DEA) believes that some Afghan heroin (70 percent of which is either consumed in or transits through Pakistan) is smuggled out of Pakistan through vessels leaving the coastal areas.[90] Since Ibrahim enjoys a nearstranglehold on smuggling activities in Karachi and has deep links in Afghanistan, D-Company profits from these activities. Although most of the profits obtained from smuggling Afghan heroin go towards personal enrichment, others go to LeT to support its operations in Kashmir and throughout India. By involving LeT in heroin smuggling, D-Company has provided LeT with an excellent opportunity for international networking as Afghan heroin serves a wide range of markets both in Asia and Europe. These transnational trafficking networks often survive political upheaval and crackdowns and would dramatically increase LeT's chances of survival even if it were abandoned by Pakistan entirely, which is unlikely. LeT could also use the nations that host their trafficking associates to hide fighters wanted by law enforcement or intelligence agencies. Clearly, by encouraging D-Company and LeT to forge ties, Pakistan made a grave strategic error by accelerating an already-worrying trend of increasing independence in LeT's decision making while Pakistan is still held responsible for the group's behavior, given its past control over it. Put simply, LeT's ties with D-Company have greatly assisted in the development of the former as an even greater security and diplomatic nightmare for Pakistan.

Chapter - 3

LeT AND D-COMPANY

In South Asia, a variety of criminal syndicates and militant groups have collaborated in international operations, and syndicates seem to have adopted ideological or religious *modus operandis* that motivate their activities, not merely cover them. Symbiotic relationships have developed with militant groups depending on organized crime for weaponry and munitions to carry out attacks and continue insurgencies. For these transfers to take place, trafficking routes have to be carefully cultivated by the syndicates, which in turn require weapons training and safe passage through militant-held territory.[91]

Dawood Ibrahim, a Sunni Muslim, was branded by the United States as an international terrorist in October 2003, for allowing al-Qaeda to use his smuggling routes to escape from Afghanistan and for assisting LeT. Further, Ibrahim and his top Lieutenant, Tiger Memon, were the key architects of the multiple bomb blasts that ripped through Bombay on March 12, 1993, targeting the Bombay Stock Exchange, Air India building, Shiv Sena Headquarters, the gold market, and the Plaza Cinema, all while avoiding areas with a predominantly Muslim population.

Thesc attacks were believed to be in response to the destruction of the Babri Masjid, a historic mosque in the Indian state of Uttar Pradesh, on December 6, 1992, and the subsequent anti-Muslim riots that followed. The blasts were designed to increase Ibrahim's support in the Muslim community by avenging the Hindu violence against Muslims. Also, D-Company's ability to smuggle in tons of explosives and enormous amounts of firepower and to recruit and train operatives in Pakistan demonstrates that the syndicate is capable of engaging in militant activity on top of its other profitdriven activities.[92]

Ibrahim's motivation to maintain his image as the protector of the Indian Muslim minority from the socalled repression of the Hindu majority led him to become involved in the Kashmir dispute. Aside from Palestine, Chechnya, and the Balkans, Kashmir is a major grievance in the Islamic world and the primary issue in South Asia. Ibrahim, through his involvement in the 1993 attacks on Bombay (his birthplace) has made it apparent that neither he nor his syndicate has an issue with attacking their own country. D-Company has well-established smuggling routes in the region, access to material, a partnership with LeT, and depends on ISI for refuge in Pakistan. Although LeT has a wide support base that spans several continents, Ibrahim is the most probable source of weaponry, given D-Company's geographic proximity to LeT operations and the syndicate's proven ability to clandestinely transfer enough weaponry to fight a small war on short notice. This is accentuated by the fact that in Pakistan there already exists a close relationship between organized criminal syndicates, narcotics, money-laundering, militant activity, and small arms trafficking.[93]

Ibrahim is believed to have resided in Pakistan since 1993 and now owns malls, luxury homes, and shipping and trucking lines that smuggle arms and heroin into India.[94] However, in exchange for his refuge in Pakistan, a percentage of D-

Company's profits were diverted to ISI-supported Islamic militant groups such as LeT. Evidence demonstrates that these links were formed in late 1993 or early 1994. Photographs of Tiger Memon posing with leaders of the Jammu and Kashmir Islamic Front (JKIF) at an ISI safe house in Muzaffarabad surfaced and served as the first proof of the involvement of mafia money in Kashmir.[95] Tanvir Ahmad Ansari, a practitioner of Unani medicine and LeT operative suspected of involvement in the 7/11 Bombay serial bombings, was tasked with strengthening relations between LeT and D-Company. Motivations for this cultivation were both tactical and strategic as LeT's partner in the Islamic Front for Jihad, al-Qaeda, expressed a desire to expand its operations in East Africa and were willing to offer cash for D-Company's networks. Ibrahim accepted al-Qaeda's offer, and Anees Ibrahim, Dawood's younger brother, made sizeable investments in the shipping industries of East Africa and the United Arab Emirates (UAE) to underwrite D-Company's narcotics trafficking activities.[96] The arrest of Syed Abdul Karim, a top LeT operative, in Mombassa, Kenya, is another demonstration of the link between LeT and D-Company as Karim was utilizing the well-established D-Company infrastructure in East Africa to avoid arrest. Ibrahim has strong relations with several wealthy traders in Mombassa, many of whom are of South Asian descent.[97] These occurrences have led some to believe that Ibrahim is the "point man" for al-Qaeda and that although Ibrahim is not an ISI agent, he is indeed an accomplice to their subversive activities.[98]

LeT, which is estimated to be responsible for 60 percent of terrorist killings in India, has been able to establish cells in several parts of the world as a result of assistance received from elements within ISI and Ibrahim's network within India and in the Gulf. There have been arrests of LeT operatives all over the world, including seven arrested by the U.S. Federal Bureau of Investigation (FBI) during Musharraf's June 2003 visit to the

United States. Even though the information was repressed in order to avoid embarrassing Musharraf, the operatives from Washington and Philadelphia were eventually charged with "stockpiling weapons and conspiring to wage jihad against India in support of terrorists in Kashmir."[99] Further, U.S. authorities claim that there are still two wanted suspects related to these arrests that are residing in Saudi Arabia.[100] D-Company has shifted some of its assets to Saudi Arabia fearing a crackdown from UAE authorities, and if LeT operatives are indeed hiding in the Sunni kingdom they are possibly doing so with Ibrahim's knowledge and assistance. Saudi money is also a primary financer of LeT's activities in Pakistan and Kashmir. As D-Company has established infrastructure in Saudi Arabia and as Riyadh's effort to stem the outward flow of terrorism from its territory have fallen short, traffic may increase as Saudi Arabia will continue to serve as a major transit point for money and fighters for conflicts in Middle Eastern hot spots such as Iraq and the Palestinian territories and also for problem zones in the Indian subcontinent. Although it is important not to adopt an alarmist stance over the potential of Saudi Arabia's enhanced role in Kashmir, it would be prudent for analysts and security personnel to monitor the situation closely.

In 2002, Ibrahim helped finance several LeT attacks in Gujarat.[101] Despite the fact that Gujarat has had its own share of communal violence, its proximity to Kashmir is a factor, and if Ibrahim is willing to assist in attacks with a more low-profile area in northern India such as Gujarat, then it is very likey that D-Company is involved in LeT's activities in Kashmir as well. The anti-Muslim violence witnessed in Gujarat is but a fraction of what has been seen in Kashmir and if incidents such as Godhra in 2002 are viewed by D-Company and LeT as sufficient justification for violent reprisals, there is no question that Kashmir qualifies to be on the receiving end of this crimeterror nexus. In addition, though investigations are ongoing, D-Company involvement in the November 2008 attacks in Mumbai is a possibility, given the syndicate's extensive resources in the city. If there was indeed any D-Company assistance, it likely took the form of logistical support. D-Company is active on both sides of the border and has both Indian and Pakistani membership with this same characteristic being witnessed in LeT.

Chapter - 4

WHY DO STATES SUPPORT TERRORISM

States that support terrorism and insurgent groups are primarily motivated by geopolitics rather than ideology, ethnic affinity, or religious sentiment. Though these less-strategic rationales at times play a crucial role in the decision of states to support irregulars, these motivations are less frequent compared to increasing regional influence, destabilizing regional rivals, or otherwise ensuring that a regime has a prominent voice in local affairs.[102] This holds true for Pakistan in that although Islamabad claims to be safeguarding the rights of its Muslim brethren in Kashmir, its interests are more motivated by larger concerns; Islamabad views the Kashmir dispute through the lens of the greater issue of overall Indo-Pak relations. Pakistan's continued support for terrorist organizations such as LeT serve a number of strategic objectives. First, it has proved to be a low-cost and, until recently, a relatively low-risk method to tie down a disproportionate number of Indian troops and make sure that the Kashmir issue remains in the spotlight. Second, by ensuring that the Indian portion of Kashmir remains an insurgency, Pakistan and its proxies have so far frustrated Indian efforts to fully incorporate Kashmir into the country. This has not only prevented India from deploying troops into other badly-needed areas, namely its Maoist-hit central and eastern provinces as well as the Northeast, but also communicates to New Delhi that, even if embroiled in a domestic crisis, Pakistan is still a force to be reckoned with. New Delhi appears to have arrived at the conclusion that it is unable to impose a military solution on the Kashmir dispute or to rely on the use of force to coerce Pakistan, something that surprises many analysts given India's clear conventional superiority. It is Pakistan's backing of irregulars, who are often unquantified variables in a conflict scenario, that has played a major role in causing New Delhi to reevaluate its past approaches toward Pakistan. In addition, Islamabad has been able to influence previous elections in J&K and still exerts influence over several J&K-based separatist leaders.

State support is an important source of strength for many insurgencies in the post-Cold War world. Outside governmental assistance helps insurgents improve their military power, recruiting base, diplomatic leverage, and other ingredients for success. Most state support tends to be provided by local governments that border the country in which a group is fighting.[103] Newer state sponsors of terrorism, such as Pakistan, can be extremely difficult to deal with as they often have a more complicated relationship with terrorist groups. In many cases, the government in question does not actively train or arm a terrorist group, but rather lets it act with relative impunity—an approach that allows the government to claim either ignorance or incapacity. Strategic rationales are the driving factor behind their actions and have several dimensions.

Making Enemies Bleed

Supporting terrorists, particularly terrorists tied to insurgent movements, can tie down large numbers of troops and security forces of an adversary and weaken the adversary's control over key parts of its territory. Pakistan's support for various groups fighting in Kashmir epitomizes this approach. Although Pakistan's ultimate aims for Kashmir are irredentist, in the short term its leaders are content to keep Indian forces occupied and prevent Kashmir's integration into the rest of India.

Subservient (Or at least Friendly) Neighbors

States are particularly concerned about their neighbors, and support for terrorists offers a form of influence. Pakistan has long supported the Taliban, as well as other groups, to maintain its influence in Afghanistan. Iran has ties to a range of militants in Iraq—including many that at times have openly criticized Baghdad—effectively giving it a veto power over decisions in parts of the country. Syria has used Hizballah and other actors to intimidate the anti-Syrian "March 14" movement in Lebanon.

Diplomatic Strength

States back terrorists as a form of diplomatic leverage in negotiations. Syria for many years used Hizballah as such a pawn in its talks over the Golan Heights. Some observers believe Iran sought to trade the senior al-Qaeda members that it is holding for U.S. concessions on members of the *Mujahedin-e Khalq* (MEK), an Iranian group opposed to the Islamic Republic, whom US forces have interned in Iraq.

Power Projection

Support for terrorists gives weak states with global ambitions influence outside their neighborhood. Iran's ties to various Palestinian groups and Hizballah gives Tehran tremendous influence in the Israeli-Palestinian theater and Lebanon, influence Iran would lack if it only relied on its weak military and economic power.

Local Power

At times a group that uses terrorism also functions as a militia, giving it tremendous influence in part of a country. Syria's cooperation with Hizballah today is driven in part by the street power offered by this strongest of all Lebanese organizations, both in Beirut and southern Lebanon. Similarly, Iran backs several factions that use terrorism, partly because they also are politically and militarily strong in key parts of Iraq close to the Iranian border.

Deterrence

Finally, supporting terrorists gives weak states a means of striking back against a militarily superior foe. Iran uses both its overseas network and its proxy killing machine in Iraq to deter the United States from increasing pressure over Tehran's nuclear program and other US-Iranian disputes.[104] Byman notes that one of the most important shifts in state sponsorship in recent years is the decline in the number of regimes with a revolutionary agenda. This shift has tremendous implications for counterterrorism in that regimes that are motivated by strategy are far more sensitive to diplomatic and economic costs as well as the risk of regime change.[105] State support for terrorism can take multiple forms, one of which is passive sponsorship and occurs when a government knowingly allows a terrorist group to raise money, enjoy a sanctuary, recruit, or otherwise flourish but does not directly aid the group itself. Passive support may prove to be the more intractable problem and has the following characteristics:

- The regime in question does not provide assistance but knowingly allows other actors in the country to aid a terrorist group.
- The regime has the capacity to stop this activity but does not do so; or has chosen not to develop this capacity.

- Passive support is often given by political parties, wealthy merchants, or other actors in society that have no formal affiliation with government.[106]

In the case of Kashmir-centered terrorist groups, Pakistan has become a passive sponsor. While disagreeing with the brazen attacks by groups such as LeT that directly target civilians in areas outside of Kashmir, successive Pakistani governments have either been unwilling or unable to meaningfully curtail their activities. Though these groups have been formally proscribed, many still continue to exist under different names and continue to enjoy indirect assistance from a variety of sources in Pakistan. When faced with pressure and accusations that Pakistan lacks the political will to crack down on terrorist groups operating on its territory, Islamabad often claims that it is actually a lack of capacity that prevents it from doing so. These events have led well-known journalist Ahmed Rashid to claim that Pakistan, and its army in particular, has still not made the necessary strategic u-turn on support to nonstate actors.[107]

States give passive support to terrorists due to factors such as domestic sympathy, a low level or perceived threat to themselves, and strategic opportunities.[108] All of these factors are present in Pakistan, especially domestic sympathy. Kashmir-based militants are often referred to as freedom fighters or "mujahideen" that are fighting for a just cause in their effort to free the Kashmiri people from perceived Indian oppression. Even many of Pakistan's leading thinkers refuse to accept the terrorism label that is placed on these groups by the West, India, and others. Needless to say, any sustained attempts to dismantle groups such as LeT have proved to be most unpopular and extremely dangerous for those involved in the implementation of the crackdown. Further, it is still widely accepted in Pakistani society that as most of the cadre of the Kashmiri groups are Pakistani and officially fighting against India, they pose no threat to the state, and further, that the recent terrorism in the country is the result of American influence in the region. Given this reality, it should not be surprising that few have anticipated LeT posing a serious threat to the security of Pakistan itself, and it also helps to explain why Islamabad has largely been reactive to recent developments.

These miscalculations are hardly unique to Pakistan. Terms such as "proxy" and "client" are often used to describe the power dynamic between Hizballah and its allies Iran and Syria. The vital resources of these states and their critical political sponsorship largely placed Hizballah in the position that it is in today. However, this image of Hizballah as a client of Iran and Syria has become obsolete due to the power base that the Shi'a group has nurtured and expanded in Lebanon and the growing political capital that it has acquired in the Middle East thanks to the perception of its military victories, namely in the war against Israel in the summer of 2006. By holding its ground against Israel, Hizballah demonstrated its capacity to shake the Lebanese and regional political landscape and resisted Israel without substantive Syrian support. By partnering with Hizballah, Damascus sought to defy isolation and reclaim its role as a pivotal power in the region and to revitalize the Asad regime. However, Hizballah has now acquired a degree of autonomy and flexibility in recent years vis-à-vis Syria, and Damascus no longer determines Hizballah's activities, something that used to guarantee the predictability and restraint that prevented all-out war. Hizballah has emerged as a more independent actor and is now able to operate in Lebanon and the wider Middle East on its own terms and has enough confidence and prestige to become more than simply a pawn for Syria to manipulate. As such, Emile El-Hokayem feels that "for strategic and ideological motives, Syria is more pro-Hizballah than Hizballah is pro-Syria."[109]

The relationship between Tehran and Hizballah is also vulnerable, though to what extent is debatable. No two actors have identical objectives and Hizballah, with its extensive presence in southern Lebanon as well as Beirut, now has its own constituencies to account for and must always be mindful of Arab nationalism and the apprehensiveness regarding Iran's rising profile in the region. In the future, it is not unrealistic to suggest that Hizballah may deem it to be in its own interest to regenerate its image, distance itself from state sponsors, and emerge as an entirely independent, self-sufficient entity that portrays itself as the Arab world's most effective response to Israel. This is much more likely if Hizballah's leadership determines that aggressive Iranian moves are damaging the group's local interests and support base in Lebanon.

Chapter - 5

LeT AND ISI

ISI was founded in 1948 by a British army officer, Major General R. Hawthorne, who was serving as the Deputy Chief of Staff in the Pakistani Army at the time. However, Field Marshal Ayub Khan, the President of Pakistan in the 1950s, greatly expanded the role of ISI in defending Pakistani interests, keeping tabs on opposition politicians, and sustaining military rule in Pakistan. Today, ISI is charged with the collection of foreign and domestic intelligence and coordination of the intelligence activities of Pakistan's three military branches. It is also responsible for surveillance over its own citizens, foreigners, the media, political parties, foreign diplomats in Pakistan, and overseas Pakistani diplomats. In addition, ISI intercepts communications and conducts covert offensive operations. Not only is it believed that ISI is not accountable to the leadership of the army, the President, or the Prime Minister, ISI is also accused of involvement in narcotics trafficking, financial crimes, and other forms of corruption. Drug money was reported to have funded the Afghan war and is believed to be currently financing Pakistan's proxy operations in Kashmir and India's

Northeast. ISI has roughly 10,000 officers and staff members, although this figure does not include informants and assets.[110]

ISI is sometimes referred to as Pakistan's secret army or invisible government and has been linked to political assassinations and the smuggling of nuclear and missile components. In addition, some claim that ISI openly backs the Taliban and has dominated Pakistan's domestic, nuclear, and foreign policies (specifically towards Afghanistan) for over 20 years.[111] At present, ISI is divided between moderates and extremist/terrorist sympathizers, thus greatly complicating its role as a NATO ally in operations against terrorist and insurgent groups in Afghanistan and Pakistan's tribal regions.[112] Further, both Pakistani officials and analysts admit that Islamic extremism is too deeply entrenched in the Pakistani military establishment to make concessions on Kashmir since elements within the army and ISI have taken control of the conflict and have begun to believe that victory is attainable if they continue to push. Lieutenant General Assad Durrani, a former ISI chief, has declared that no border has ever been drawn without blood being spilled.[113] However, it should also be noted that Pakistan's continued involvement is not simply driven by extremism, but rather by a range of other strategic calculations. Most critically, Pakistan's main rivers originate in the Indian portion of Kashmir.[114] Further, if India can demonstrate that it is capable of governing a Muslim-majority region, it undermines Pakistan's fundamental reason for existence; the need for a homeland for South Asia's Muslims.

Several quotes from Hamid Gul, an outspoken and highly controversial retired general and former ISI director, possibly provide some first hand insight into ISI ideology regarding Kashmir:

> Who is Pervez Musharraf to say we should stop jihad, when the Koran says it and when the United Nations Charter backs it up? Musharraf says: "Stop the jihad,"

> do this, that and the other. No, no, no. He cannot. There is a clear-cut Koranic injunction.
>
> Armed resistance of the oppressed people, of the persecuted people, of the enslaved people—that jihad has the UN sanction.[115]

It is hard to imagine that this sense of ideological and political legitimacy at the top of an organization such as ISI has not trickled down to middle and lower ranking officers. This open contradiction of Musharraf's statements and Pakistan's official Kashmir policy is a clear indication of the boldness of ISI, which is often referred to as a state within a state that sometimes makes its own decisions and is not accountable to the political leadership or civil society. It is said that Pakistan is governed by the "Three As": Army, Allah, and America. As Washington has refused to chide Pakistan's use of irregulars in Kashmir until fairly recently, and continued to provide Islamabad with billions of dollars worth of aid and weaponry, extremists in ISI and its Kashmir-based patrons likely felt that they were on the right side of all three. The deployment of a few thousand militants by ISI has proven to be cost effective as they have managed to pin down nearly a third of the Indian army and have enabled Islamabad to degrade India's conventional superiority and thereby restrict India's capacity to engage in conflicts elsewhere.[116] The Pakistani military is also determined to obtain revenge against India for encouraging separatism in the former East Pakistan in 1971, and although there have been rifts between the Generals and the Pakistani government, elements within ISI still provide assistance to LeT.[117] Some have even gone as far to say that LeT's evolution to becoming a major Pakistani group operating in Kashmir is largely attributed to Saeed's close ties to ISI and the Pakistani military.[118]

ISI is believed to run some of LeT's training camps and is accused of having been the terrorist group's primary financer and supporter. Based upon these facts, some find it highly ironic that the ISI was entrusted to investigate LeT's role in the failed plot to simultaneously blow up to as many as ten airplanes on transatlantic routes.[119] ISI is estimated to be running around 256 (the methodology for reaching this figure is unknown) modules across India and pushing LeT to become the most dynamic militant group that operates in J&K, New Delhi, Bombay, Bangalore, Hyderabad, Varanasi, and Kolkata.[120] Lieutenant General Mahmood Ahmed, the then-Director General of ISI, was reported to have attended an April 2001 LeT-sponsored conference in Muridke that saw a resolution passed which charged its India-based cadre to capture and destroy Hindu temples and place the flag of Islam on top of their ruins.[121]

Many militant groups, including LeT, operate freely in Pakistan-held Kashmir, and the area has become a safe haven for many foreign fighters who have fled Afghanistan. Also, fighters that have trained at ISI run camps in Afghanistan are increasingly returning to Kashmir, where many of them have their roots. (Some camps that used to be based in the disputed region were moved to Afghanistan by ISI in order to ensure their continued operation.) While ISI and the Pakistani Army selectively pursue al-Qaeda operatives within Pakistan's tribal areas, many of the training grounds that house Kashmiri fighters remain largely untouched.[122] This development indicates that ISI seeks to keep the Kashmir-based fighters as a reserve force in the event of increased tensions with India and has not abandoned their support as Pakistan has pledged to do numerous times. However, ISI has made a critical error in viewing groups such as LeT as static organizations that will not develop independently or stray from their initial focus. Ironically, the longer ISI assists LeT in its operations in Kashmir and within the Indian Union, the less influence it will have over the organization in the future. If present trends prevail, future efforts to shut down LeT, no matter how sincere, will inevitably result in failure as the group will have become multinational with a wide variety of state and nonstate sponsors and sources of funding, and will have fighters and other resources dispersed throughout several areas.

Pakistan will not cease support to groups such as LeT until there is a formal resolution to the Kashmir dispute.[123] However, the resolution of the Kashmir conflict in the short to medium term is an unlikely prospect for a number of reasons. First, India has ruled out the possibility of withdrawing troops entirely and has refused seemingly less risky options such as reducing troop numbers or removing them from certain areas such as the Siachen glacier. New Delhi has even declined Islamabad's offer to validate troop positions. Further, the recent drop in the number of infiltrations across the Line of Control (LOC) and overall militant activity in Kashmir are more of a reflection of ISI focusing its attention elsewhere, such as tribal regions along the Afghanistan-Pakistan border, rather than a permanent strategic shift or loss of interest. Third, a series of erroneous decisions on behalf of President Musharraf (for example, the decision to sack Pakistan's independent-minded chief justice only to see him reinstated), combined with internal unrest following the raid of Lal Masjid and the looming threat of a unilateral US military strike against al-Qaeda leadership in the tribal regions, placed Musharraf in an embattled state. As a result, he did not have the support within the army or ISI to push through any significant change in Pakistan's approach to Kashmir despite official offerings of demilitarization, joint management, etc. As such, Pakistan's support for LeT will continue to serve as a destabilizing factor in the region and as a major irritant to bilateral diplomacy between New Delhi and Islamabad.

Chapter - 6

THE FUTURE OF ISLAMIST TERRORISM IN INDIA

Indian security forces have been witnessing a disturbing trend in the indigenization of several Pakistan and Bangladesh-based militant groups that is believed to have led to the formation of the Indian Mujahideen (IM). IM is believed to have a substantial number of Indian nationals within its ranks, and its recent attacks were likely carried out by Indians, something that runs counter to the conventional wisdom that terrorist attacks in India are invariably carried out by foreigners, usually Pakistanis. Much of this reformation likely involves the ISI, with the goal of establishing native cells that mostly operate autonomously but will still occasionally take directives from abroad.[124] These cells will likely be highly difficult to detect as they are small and consist of Indians with first-hand knowledge of the country that do not appear foreign in any way. Further, any ruling party in New Delhi will have difficulty enacting tougher legislation to combat the problem for fear of losing the Muslim vote. India is also at a disadvantage as its intelligence services lack Muslim personnel and have become too dependent upon technology at the expense of human intelligence. Lastly, India needs to acknowledge that many Muslims are treated as second-class citizens in the country and have suffered from selective justice and discrimination for decades, and that this does wonders for the recruitment efforts of groups such as IM.

Although ISI, LeT, and others have assets in India, D-Company's network is far more extensive. As elements within ISI further their agenda of developing and spinning off terrorist groups within India while the civilian leadership pledges to crack down on these same organizations, they will come to rely more heavily on D-Company infrastructure in ventures such as ensuring the safe entry and exit of foreign terrorists and the provision of safe houses, clean phones, weapons, explosives, and other related material. They will also need D-Company operatives to reconnoiter targets and manage ISI's relationships with corrupt officials within India. Through D-Company, extremists in ISI may be able to establish even greater distance between themselves and the myriad of terrorist groups, namely LeT, that jeopardize Indian stability. D-Company also benefits from this partnership as it allows it to assist in avenging the deaths of Muslims in areas such as Gujarat, the scene of a serial bombing in July 2008. D-Company had long sought to carry out an operation in Gujarat following the massacre of over 1,000 Muslims by Hindu mobs in 2002, and its participation was likely.

November 2008 Mumbai Attacks

The Mumbai attacks displayed a level of advanced planning that shows a considerable evolution in Islamist terrorist groups in South Asia. There were multiple targets within an urban environment. Highly trained and armed terrorists organized into small teams that targeted Americans, Britons, and Jews, as well as Indians, with the major final showdown occurring in hotels, a favorite target of al-Qaeda.[125] The masterminds of these attacks were sophisticated in their strategic thinking and the operation was able to capture and hold international attention while seeking to exacerbate communal tensions. They also aimed to provoke a crisis between India and Pakistan, thereby prompting Pakistan to shift troops from the Federally Administered Tribal Area (FATA) and the Northwest Frontier Province (NWFP) to its frontier with India. This would have taken pressure off the Taliban, al-Qaeda, and other groups operating along the Afghan frontier. After these attacks, the Mumbai attackers further burnished their terrorist credentials and now rival al-Qaeda in reputation. This operation also foreshadows a continuing terrorist campaign in India.[126] However, an attack of this magnitude required a safe haven from which they could plan, train, and communicate without fear of disruption. Given the heightened sense of security in India, such a safe haven is unlikely to be established in the country. As such, any future spectaculars on Indian soil are likely to originate from overseas in the short to medium term. The fact that India's Maoists have been unable to execute any kind of operation that approximates the 2008 Mumbai attacks is a case in point. All of the facilities attacked were soft targets, and at no point during the attack did the terrorists attempt to overcome armed guards. The terrorists attacked predominantly unguarded targets; and even at places where they could expect security forces, reconnaissance informed them that those forces could be easily overcome as they were only lightly armed.[127] Terrorist groups will continue to focus on soft targets in India that offer high body counts and have iconic value. Nationally and internationally recognized venues that offer ease of access, certainty of tactical success, and the ability to kill in large quantities will likely guide future target selection. Further, as public surface transportation offers terrorists easily accessible, dense populations in confined environments, it will likely remain the most common form of attack.[128]

Some observers claim that the Mumbai attackers felt that they were somehow going to get out alive. This view has been strengthened by reports that this belief was shared by the sole surviving terrorist.[129] If accurate, this is problematic for India as the quality of future *fidayeen*-style terrorists is likely to be higher than standard suicide bombers. If the chance of survival is present, no matter how slim, these types of attacks can potentially attract highly motivated terrorists keen to engage in extended operations that are guaranteed to gain international media attention due to their shock value. Participation in a *fidayeen* attack can bring prestige to the individual as well as the group as it is considered a more courageous act than suicide by many within the larger Islamist terrorist community.

The two-man team that stormed the Trident-Oberoi Hotel called the news media, claiming that seven terrorists were in the building and demanding that India release all "mujahideen" in Indian prisons in exchange for the release of hostages.[130] A key question here is whether this was a prime objective of the operation, or if it was something more spontaneous. It is of note that India has released terrorists in exchange for hostages in the past, with the most notable release being JeM's Masood Azhar in 1999. Though this demand appeared to be hastily arranged and possibly generated on the spot, the release of imprisoned comrades could become a driver behind future operations. Such events would hardly be unprecedented in India as the Maoists have engaged in successful jail-breaks freeing hundreds of their members.

The dispersal of the attackers into separate teams indicates an effort to reduce operational risk. Once the attack commenced, the failure or elimination of any single team would not have put the other teams out of action. This type of operation, where attackers assault and penetrate deep into the target and try to kill as many as possible, has been a LeT hallmark against Indian forces in Kashmir.[131] Fortunately for India, this capability is beyond IM at this point in time as it is still somewhat of a disjointed organization in the consolidation stage. However, over time IM can develop it with a safe haven, in Pakistan or otherwise. The recent scaling up of IM's campaign demonstrates clear intent to take their operations to the next level and if regular contact with groups like LeT are maintained, more destructive attacks with multiple sophisticated objectives are a real possibility. In addition, Indian security forces have made the startling discovery of at least six training camps within India itself.[132]

According to the testimony of the surviving terrorist, the goal of the operation was to kill as many people as possible. However, when compared to the 2006 Mumbai train attack, or the 1993 Mumbai bombings, casualties in the 2008 operation were lower as bombs were not the primary weapon. Indiscriminate bombings, namely those in London and Madrid, have been criticized in Islamist terrorist circles as being contrary to the Islamic code of warfare. As such, it is likely that by relying on shooters, this 2008 attack would appear to be more selective even though the majority of victims were still civilian. This perception of selectivity was further underscored by the terrorists' search for Americans and Britons at the hotel, and the killings at the Jewish Chabad Centre. It also enabled the attackers to engage the police and soldiers in what could be portrayed as a heroic last stand. Security could have been another factor; based on the patterns of previous attacks, Indian authorities were focused on truck bombs at hotels while rail security focused on trying to keep bombs off trains as opposed to keeping armed assailants out of the actual train stations.[133] Following the most recent attacks, LeT is anticipating another round of target hardening in India, and Mumbai in particular, and will have to innovate if it wants to maintain its position within the South Asian terrorist community. As LeT thinking evolves, it will seek to carry out attacks that have chain reaction-type effects that remain long after the attack itself. These effects alter behavior and ensure that a sense of fear remains, something that will require the expertise of an in-country partner such as D-Company. Though LeT is a distinctive outfit is its own right, it is likely in tune to international best practices and is aware that one of the most effective ways to weaken a regime and damage a nation's long-term development is through consistently hitting economic targets. Key drivers of the Indian economy, namely IT, financial services, and steel manufacturing, should be viewed as potential high-value targets. Despite the horrific human losses inflicted by LeT gunmen in Mumbai, the permanent damage to India's economy was minimal, and it did not take Mumbai long to return to its normal state. Similar events were witnessed following the train bombings in 2006. Given LeT's proven ability to learn and evolve as an organization, this lesson it not likely to be lost on them. However, IM is not able to carry out this level of operations though its LeT patrons are keen to see them develop the capability. As such, the onus for carrying out mass casualty attacks in India will remain on LeT with the assistance of D-Company's logistical support network for the time being.

Terrorists have proven themselves capable of analyzing current security measures, devising new tactics to circumvent them, and doing the unexpected. The terrorists also demonstrated that even with simple tactics and low-tech weapons they are still able to produce vastly disproportionate results. Further, the success of the Mumbai attackers in paralyzing a large city and commanding the attention of the world's news media for nearly 3 days will encourage similar operations in the future. Terrorists will continue to effectively embed themselves among civilians, taking hostages, and using them as human shields to impede responders and maximize collateral casualties.[134]

Terrorist attacks are intended to cause fear, but also to inspire other terrorist constituencies and attract recruits. By succeeding, which in this case means humiliating the Indian security services, causing large-scale death and destruction, and garnering international media coverage, terrorists hope to attract both Pakistani and Indian recruits to their cause.[135] A critical factor will be the overall response of Indian Muslim "fence-sitters" who are disillusioned with contemporary India and their place in society but have not yet resorted to taking up arms. Given the legitimacy that many Pakistanis assign to the Kashmir dispute, LeT is not likely to experience recruitment difficulties in the near future, but if the group is to achieve its objectives in India, it will need more capable domestic recruits.

Two alleged Indian LeT operatives, Fahim Ansari and Sabauddin Ahmed, were arrested and accused of scouting for the attacks.[136] Indian nationals are also believed to have possibly helped with the prepositioning of supplies. According to one account, at the Taj Hotel Indian commandos discovered a backpack containing seven loaded AK-47 magazines, 400 spare rounds, four hand grenades, and various documents that may have been placed beforehand .[137]

New Delhi claims that all of the Mumbai attackers were members of LeT, received advanced military training in Pakistan, and arrived in India by boat. Although met with initial skepticism by some, these claims seem to have been validated. However, it should be noted that to carry out an attack of such scale, considerable reconnaissance was required on these symbolic targets, something that would have taken months or even longer and could not have happened without in country assets. In addition, although the devastating effectiveness of this operation was due to its lack of many interconnected moving parts, it was still a substantial logistical exercise, especially regarding target location. The Taj, Oberoi, Chhatrapati Shivaji rail station, and maybe even the Leopold Café were not difficult to identify, but the deliberate targeting of Nariman House and inside the Jewish center likely could not have occurred without local knowledge.

This is not to suggest that the operation was not mostly a LeT venture, but much like the serial bombings in Mumbai in 1993, such an ambitious plan could not have been completely developed outside of India and only by Pakistanis. As stated earlier, LeT, D-Company, and its handlers have been pursuing a policy of indigenization of Islamist terrorism in India, meaning that as LeT cells expand throughout the country, they obtain more Indian cadre and link up with like-minded groups such as the SIMI. Indian authorities believe that this is how IM was formed along with segments of other groups based in Bangladesh. However, without the native component, the IM would have difficulty functioning.

So why are Indian Muslims now willing to be involved in attacks that kill their fellow citizens on a massive scale and try to damage their own economy by hitting hotels and other commercial sites like bazaars? There are many analysts who attribute this to pervasive and systematic discrimination against Muslims in Indian society. They claim that Muslims die earlier, are less healthy, and do not have the same access to education as their Hindu counterparts. However, such disparities are also witnessed in minority communities in many countries, including the United States, although they do not resort to taking up arms against their own counury.

A major contributing factor for Islamist terrorism in India is the selective nature of Indian justice when it comes to prosecuting acts of communal violence. For example, India relentlessly pushes for the extradition of Dawood Ibrahim from Pakistan for his involvement in the 1993 Mumbai attacks while many of those who perpetrated or instigated the 2002 Gujarat riots, in which scores of Muslim innocents were killed, have not been brought to justice. Contradictions such as these serve as powerful motivators, while evidence is also starting to emerge that some Indian Muslims are beginning to identify with the Kashmir dispute.

This is something that could prove disastrous if not addressed.

Many Indians are convinced that LeT is sponsored by the Pakistani government, and as such, India is likely to respond to these types of attacks in a manner that holds Islamabad directly responsible.[138] LeT and their allies are aware of this and will seek to actively exploit the situation in order to reverse any positive momentum in relations between India and Pakistan. If New Delhi believes a state hand is behind LeT spectaculars, its response will be more bellicose thus exacerbating tensions and, ironically, assisting militants to achieve their objectives. Further, if India conducted military attacks on suspected terrorist training bases in Pakistan, it would provoke anger and strengthen Pakistani hardliners.[139] It would also increase public sympathy for many of the Kashmir centered groups, namely LeT, as it would further bolster their image of being on the front line against a hostile India.

Chapter - 7

FUTURE DIRECTIONS OF THE INDIAN MUJAHIDEEN

The fundamental difference between the attacks by Islamists in Kashmir and the more recent attacks in India is that, while the previous operations were carried out by foreigners or hardcore locals, recent attacks involve individuals and cells from a broader section of India's Muslim population. The growing popularity of the anti-Muslim agenda of the Hindu nationalists is causing greater communal polarization and prompting many Indian Muslims to support the concept of Muslim self-defense more strongly. Recognizing the situation, Pakistan and the ISI are believed to have used D-Company and SIMI to provide the contacts, safe houses, and front organizations needed to enable LeT, JeM, and HUJI-B to become all-India threats. Indian security officials cite the terrorist attacks in Bangalore, Ahmedabad, and Surat (July 25-27, 2008) as recent examples of this nexus at work.[140] However, these attacks are more reactive in nature and driven by anger and feelings of alienation rather than the desire to achieve complex political objectives. This type of urban terrorism likely does not require much, if any, planning and training outside of India and, if conducted in isolation and not part of a coordinated campaign, the long-term effects are not incredibly severe. However, as demonstrated by the Provisional Irish Republican Army (PIRA), if IM can transform these somewhat isolated attacks into a consistent campaign, they can cause long-lasting damage even if their tactics do not advance considerably. It is possible that this is actually the intention of IM's foreign patrons at present.

In the wake of the Mumbai bombings in 2006, LeT came under intense pressure from the Musharraf regime to scale back its offensive operations against India. As such, Zakiur Rahman Lakhvi and other LeT commanders prodded their Indian counterparts to set up a self-sustaining network in India. On the eve of attacking three court buildings in Uttar Pradesh in November 2007, the group finally named itself the Indian Mujahideen.[141] IM was still very much a work in progress when LeT had to scale back its assistance rather unexpectedly. This stunted IM's growth and likely caused LeT to modify its expectations for the group. In the early stages, it appears that LeT, with D-Company assistance, aimed to turn IM into their India-based crack force that remained completely obedient. However, once it became clear that these aims were unrealistic, LeT had to improvise and accept an autonomous IM that takes occasional directives from LeT and its allies outside of India. Though this helps to hide foreign involvement, it also greatly lessens the amount of command and control that can be exerted over IM by LeT.

Key leaders of IM escaped a nationwide police hunt which led to the arrest of over 80 of its operatives in six states in 2008. Police services across India claim that they have credible intelligence that IM is planning further strikes and dozens of Indian terrorists have received training in Pakistan.[142] Even if these reports are accurate, recent attacks by IM were not particularly sophisticated and did not require many specialized skills. Though importing certain components such as bomb-making skills and financial assistance are real possibilities, it is critical that India does not overemphasize the importance of Pakistan and Bangladesh with regards to IM. Even without foreign assistance, IM can still carry out attacks though not at the level of LeT.

Kashmir—Expanding the Conflict Theater

Faced with India's conventional superiority, Pakistan believed that its interests were favored by a military equation that saw the largest number of Indian troops diverted and towards internal security operations and away from a possible Indian strike force aimed at Pakistan. Islamabad also believed that it could calibrate and control this policy, an assessment that generally held until the Afghan jihad ended with the fall of Najibullah's communist regime in Kabul in April 1992. Although Islamabad's policy remained constant, several other external factors made J&K an increasingly volatile flashpoint. First, the victory over the Union of Soviet Socialist Republics (USSR) inspired Kashmiri militants to believe that New Delhi could also be beaten. Second, a moderate number of Pakistani and Indian Kashmiris received training and combat experience in Afghanistan during the war against the Soviets and believed that they were ready to fight Indian forces. Third, Islamist NGOs from the Arabian Peninsula looked for post-Afghan causes to support and Kashmiri separatists figured prominently. Lastly, after al-Qaeda's formation in 1988, it took a strong interest in the Kashmiri militants and began to assist them after the Soviet withdrawal. Each of these factors lessened Islamabad's ability to effectively regulate the violence in Kashmir and thereby limit chances of a military confrontation with India. Even if Islamabad tightened the spigot, assistance came from other sources.[143]

Pakistan's covert operations alone would not have posed a threat to Indian security and stability, but rising anti-Hindu sentiments among India's 150 million strong Muslim community have complemented Pakistani operations and enhanced the threat posed to India's communal harmony and economy, something that increases the likelihood of an unintended India- Pakistan war. Nonetheless, this situation was still manageable, but with the rise of Hindu nationalism and cultural chauvinism, or Hindutva, the situation has become more severe. The rapid growth of the Bharatiya Janafa Party (BJP—a Hindu nationalist political party) and the simultaneous expansion of the Mumbai-based Shiv Sena (Army of Shiva) began to challenge the secular credentials of the Indian state in a manner that was openly anti-Muslim. By the late 1990s Hindu nationalist leaders were pushing for the imposition of domestic policies, namely in the area of counterterrorism, that widened the Hindu-Muslim communal divide and created a permissive environment for the development of anti-Hindu Islamist militancy in India. Further, since the US-led invasion of Afghanistan in 2001, Pakistan has continued its covert operations in Kashmir, and as a response to Indian moves in Afghanistan, aims to create an insurgent/terrorist capability across India to attack the booming economy.[144]

After lying low for a few months following the November 2008 Mumbai carnage, and the subsequent crackdown on its Pakistan-based camps and leadership, LeT began scaling its operations back up in J&K. LeT fighters engaged Indian regulars of 1 Para and 6 Battalion Rashtriya Rifles (a counterterrorism paramilitary unit created in 1990 for use in Kashmir) in a 5-day firefight beginning on March 20, 2009, in the Shamasbari forest range of Kupwara district near the LoC. LeT claimed responsibility for the ambush on an army patrol and the following encounter in which 17 militants and eight soldiers (including a major) were killed. The Indian Army attributed its losses to the technical sophistication of the insurgents and their use of global positioning systems (GPS) in the densely forested region. India claims that it has also recovered snow gear, advanced maps, satellite phones, rations, and medical supplies.[145] This equipment points to continued involvement by elements within Pakistan's security forces. Following the admission of involvement in LeT by the sole surviving Mumbai terrorist, the group's image suffered tremendously throughout Pakistan as well as Kashmir, as it risked pulling the decades-old dispute into the greater war on terror framework, something that would allow India to become even more inflexible regarding negotiations on the issue. LeT appears keenly aware that its core source of legitimacy stems from its fight against Indian security forces in Kashmir, and that this cannot be compromised. Wisely, LeT waited for the regional security environment to settle somewhat before reengaging the Kashmir theater. These actions sought to clearly communicate to New Delhi and the Kashmiris that LeT remains resolutely focused on Kashmir while also attempting to signal to ordinary Pakistanis and their allies in the security forces that LeT is still a reliable partner that seeks to forward Pakistani objectives vis-à-vis India. By continuing to fight in Kashmir, LeT makes it more difficult and politically unpopular to crack down on its activities in Pakistan despite the fact that its other actions in India and elsewhere clearly undermine Pakistani security.

After recently overhauling its infrastructure in J&K, LeT has vowed to continue its operations against security forces and vital installations in the state. Further, unconfirmed reports state that LeT has opened up more camps in Muzzafarabad, Mirpur, and Kotli for the fresh recruitment and training of new fighters and has replaced the commanders that were taken into Pakistani custody. As such, many have raised questions regarding how LeT was able to bounce back so quickly even after Pakistan's so-called crackdown following the Mumbai attacks.[146] Reports about training camps are often exaggerated and nearly impossible to verify. However, until Pakistan's border dispute with India as well as Afghanistan is resolved, Islamabad is not likely to drop its support for irregulars, as Pakistan has come to view many of them as an insurance policy against what Islamabad assesses to be hostile neighbors. Unless these fundamental issues are addressed, Pakistan is likely to continue on this ultimately self destructive path much to the detriment of regional and international security.

Veteran Kashmiri guerrilla commander Ilyas Kashmiri is overseeing the development of the new "neo-Taliban" strategy in Afghanistan which seeks to complement the traditional guerrilla war of the Kandahari clan in southwestern Afghanistan and suicide operations in and around Kabul and in southeastern Afghanistan. These neo-Taliban also intend to spread chaos throughout Pakistan and India through kidnappings, high profile attacks, and other asymmetric tactics. After this, they intend to go a step further by actively engaging security forces once military operations are diverted by the chaos that has been caused. The Arab and former Kashmiri fighters that form the bulk of the neo-Taliban have been fighting under the command and strategy of the Taliban in Afghanistan but have now formed into a separate entity.[147] Given the background of this group and the nature of terrorism and insurgency in the region, this organization likely has links to Kashmir and can shift back to that theater if they become disenchanted in Afghanistan or if the conflict ends. In the event that this group returns to Kashmir and greater India, it will be even more capable after spending years engaging American and NATO forces in Afghanistan.

The Mehsud tribe is believed to provide base camps for these fighters and also raises money. It is estimated that between November 2008 and April 2009 alone, Tehrik-i-Taliban Pakistan's (TTP) network in Karachi generated at least 250 million rupees (US $3.1 million) through various operations, including extorting fuel contractors for coalition troops in Afghanistan and ransom money from kidnappings and threats.

These proceeds have been used to open up new guerrilla training camps in both Pakistan and Afghanistan.[148] TTP has links with mainstream LeT, so these fighters in Afghanistan can hardly be viewed as insulated from the Kashmir insurgency. TTP also uses LeT and other infrastructure of the Punjabi-dominated groups to attack in settled areas of Pakistan such as Lahore and Islamabad as well as rural southern Punjab. This will inevitably have an impact on India, and with additional safe havens to plan and train, another spectacular attack by LeT or a related group on Indian territory cannot be ruled out. Pakistan's Punjabi militants are highly trained and have become battled hardened after years of fighting in India and J&K. In such an event, there is no guarantee that American diplomacy could prevent a major conventional war.

It is believed that the March 2009 attacks on a police academy in Lahore were carried out by militants who have been associated with LeT and Harakat-ul-Jihadi- Islami Pakistan (HUJI-P). Security sources claim that the group travelled to Lahore from a militant camp in the North Waziristan town of Razmak. After killing a number of cadets and taking many others hostage, the lead militants are reported to have slipped away, leaving behind a few men to keep the shootout with security forces going for 8 hours. The fugitives most likely then travelled to cities in southern Punjab, namely Multan. Intelligence agencies maintain that some of the militants came from Punjab and spoke Urdu, Punjabi, and Seraiki, even though FATA based TTP claimed responsibility for the attack.[149] These attacks and the attack on the Sri Lankan cricket team in Lahore represent some dangerous muscle flexing by Pakistan's original jihadis, mostly Punjabis trained by the military in the 1990s as the first line of defense for the country, especially in Kashmir. These militants remained neutral after the US invasion of Afghanistan in 2001 and only joined the Taliban's fight against foreign forces in Afghanistan in 2004 through the provision of training and logistics.

However, they did not involve themselves in the hostilities in the tribal areas.[150] This has now clearly changed, thus rendering any distinctions between militants even more indisputably obsolete and demonstrates that Pakistan's outfits, including its supposed allies like LeT, have made a strategic decision to escalate their campaigns in the country even if it pushes Pakistan to the brink.

LeT's parent outfit, Jamaat-ud-Dawa (JuD), is considered to be the best organized Islamic charity in South Asia with a social network unmatched by other Islamic groups or militant outfits. By responding to social and economic ills under the platform of Islamic social justice, groups like JuD have done extremely well in meeting the population's expectations in times of crises or natural disasters and winning their loyalty as a result. Through these provisions of social services, JuD is able to connect in a way that the Pakistani state cannot. This puts pressure on the state and also prevents external actors from exploiting the local population to steer them away from the Islamists' camp. In doing so, JuD, and by extension LeT, are able to expand their organization through social networking. This allows them to maintain a level of independence and qualify as legitimate authorities to a population that increasingly perceives the civilian government as corrupt and weak in the face of Western demands.[151] This is a major impediment to shutting down LeT infrastructure as it could create a massive vacuum that would likely be filled by another nonstate actor. By thinking strategically, LeT and JuD have taken steps to ensure that any effort to uproot them will be most painful for society and the government.

LeT seems to have a heightened awareness of the power of emotions and a need to continue to engage in surprising moves to maintain their elevated status. LeT/JuD also seeks to appeal to a global audience despite being a local group, something that has prompted comparisons with al-Qaeda. It also attracts members from outside of Pakistan and has infrastructure in Central Asia and the Arab World.[152] This likely has much to do with LeT's inflated ambitions, but it still cannot afford to shift its primary focus from Kashmir and India. For this, LeT has to maintain its infrastructure in J&K, carry out innovative spectaculars in India, and continue to nurture IM.

Assam: The Next Front?

The October 30, 2008, Assam blasts claimed 85 lives and injured nearly 500 people. Sophisticated weaponry and unknown smuggling networks were used to carry out these attacks as opposed to the relatively crude locally assembled explosives used elsewhere in India such as New Delhi, Mumbai, Hyderabad, and Varanasi. The bombs used in Assam have raised concerns over the region's porous borders as well as links between local separatist militant groups, especially from Bangladesh and Myanmar. Security experts say that the car and motorcycle bombs used were often laden with over 80 kilograms of RDX, well beyond the capability of domestic separatist outfits such as the United Liberation Front of Assam (ULFA) or the National Democratic Front of Bodoland (NDFB).[153] Prior to the bombings, there had been brutal anti-Bengali/Muslim riots and communal tensions were high.

India's Home Ministry believes that HUJI-B was involved in the Assam bombings and that the group maintains close ties with IM. In Assam, HUJI-B is believed to utilize its close connections with illegal immigrants from Bangladesh for new recruits, safe houses, and logistical support, and reports suggest that the Indian government has identified 46 points along the border with Bangladesh that are being used as exit and entry points by HUJI-B.[154] Bangladesh is facing a major yet little-publicized national security challenge from terrorist groups.

Unfortunately, a common perception exists amongst the greater counterterrorism community that Bangladeshi terrorist groups do not have significant linkages with groups outside the country and therefore do not pose a challenge to international security. Put simply, the common viewpoint is that these groups are waging an internal struggle and are not linked to global terrorism.

Chapter - 8

RADICALIZATION OF SECURITY PERSONNEL IN BANGLADESH

While investigations are still underway into the Bangladesh Rifles (BDR—a paramilitary border security force) mutiny that took place in February 2009, there have been allegations made in several quarters, including by the minister responsible for coordinating the investigations, about a possible involvement by Bangladesh-based Jamaat-ul Mujahideen Bangladesh and other terrorist organizations. If the suspicion proves to be true, this would have serious implications for Bangladesh's national security. Many of the bodies of the Bangladeshi Army officers that were killed in the mutiny were mutilated in a barbaric, brutal fashion. Does this point towards a possible radicalization of certain members of the security forces? If that is the case, then that would raise serious concerns and would require Bangladeshi authorities to have a hard look at the internal oversight procedures of the security apparatus. It is also to note that over 1,800 BDR personnel still have not returned for duty and are dispersed throughout the country. Despite Operation REBEL HUNT, some of these deserters are not likely to be located. Potentially radicalized paramilitary and regular soldiers are especially dangerous for a number of reasons. First, they tend to be well trained in combat techniques and the use of weaponry. Second, as they have previously served in the armed forces or paramilitaries, they have knowledge of the layout of various facilities and the strengths and weaknesses of the security forces. Third, their actions can serve as a powerful motivator for many fence-sitters, who are also disillusioned with their positions, as well as with society at large. Finally, extremist ex-soldiers may have a line of communication open with still-serving personnel. These soldiers not only constitute a large group of well-trained men, but they also may have a significant portion of the weapons and ammunition that were looted from BDR during the mutiny.[155]

With extremist groups now equipped with the necessary resources, Bangladesh and India have to contend with the possibility of the ranks of existing groups mushrooming or witnessing a dangerous proliferation of self-starter groups, either of which will have knock-on effects in India, especially in nearby areas where there is communal tension and a conducive environment like Assam. Further, IM is not likely to have remained idle while massive amounts of weapons flowed out of BDR headquarters, and Bangladesh's border defenses were also down. As such, IM's biggest operational upgrade may come from Bangladesh instead of Pakistan.

Bangladesh-Afghanistan Connection

A fact that is often ignored is that the senior leadership of Bangladeshi terrorist groups such as JMB and HUJI-B took an active part in the armed resistance against the Soviet Union. The leaders of HUJI-B saw action in several provinces in Afghanistan, and it was during this time that they came into close contact with individuals who later went on to assume important leadership positions in militant groups across the South Asian region and beyond.[156] For around a decade, these individuals participated side by side against the USSR, and these relationships did not likely fade following the Soviet withdrawal. In addition to JMB and HUJI-B, the senior leadership of the vast majority of Islamist terrorist groups in South Asia still includes individuals who fought in the Afghan anti-Soviet resistance. Therefore, there is a very real possibility that Bangladeshi terrorist leaders are able to leverage the long-term relationships they forged with their counterparts in South Asia and possibly the Middle East, and can translate this into a strong collaborative operational relationship between their groups. The bonds that were initially formed in Afghanistan are more than likely to have been further cemented over the years as they continue to engage in activities that are driven by the same ideological reasoning.[157] As such, it is vital that this phenomenon be examined, and that the transnational linkages of Bangladeshi terror groups are adequately understood if counterterrorism policies, strategies, and tactics are to be effective.

Different Enemies, Common Justifications

A concept that frequently appears in the strategic communications put forward by South Asian terrorist groups is the comparison of everything that they stand against with *Taghoot* or the force of evil. Referring to some verses in the Quran and interpreting it to suit their requirements, these groups try to portray their enemies as alongside the forces of evil. The same reasoning is used by JMB, Pakistan-based LeT and Jaish-e-Mohammad, and a number of other Islamist terrorist organizations across South Asia. The forces that these groups claim to fight against are diverse. For example, while JMB is fighting Dhaka to establish a puritanical Islamic state in Bangladesh, LeT and JeM are fighting against the Indian state using Kashmir as their main justification. However, while the targets are different, the ideological justifications are usually the same. They also share an almost pathological disdain for the West, and the United States in particular. When JMB sends a message, while the Bangladeshi state and society remains the main enemy, the West and the United States are also targeted. Further, HUJI-B espouses the same extremist Deobandi ideology which inspires JeM and other groups in the region.[158]

Understanding the Threat from Bangladeshi Groups

While distinct organizations, both JMB and HUJI-B share some striking similarities. In Pakistan, even groups such as Tehrik-i-Taliban Pakistan and others which are actively engaged in hostilities with Pakistan's security forces still espouse nationalist rhetoric and offered to stand and fight with the Pakistan Army in the event of an Indian attack following the carnage in Mumbai in November 2008. They are also in lockstep with the position of many Pakistanis regarding the Kashmir dispute. However, HUJI-B and JMB are fundamentally against all tenets of the Bangladeshi state and society and seek to overthrow the secular government, replace the Western-style court system, and establish a Taliban-style state in Bangladesh. It should be remembered that several of HUJI-B's most senior leaders are veterans of the Afghan conflict against the Soviet Union, and that Osama bin Laden provided critical financial backing during the group's infant stages. Despite being a much younger organization that is believed to have been formed around 1998, JMB's ideology and vision for Bangladesh's future does not differ dramatically from HUJI-B's. JMB is an extremely formidable outfit as was demonstrated by its ability to carry out over 400 coordinated bomb blasts within one hour in all but one district in Bangladesh. Further, the threat posed by JMB as well as HUJI-B recently forced Sheikh Hasina to curtail her travel plans following her recent election.

Among the counterterrorism community, while Indian and Pakistan terror groups get a lot of attention, the groups operating in Bangladesh are often believed to be substantially weaker and operating mainly withlocal motivations.[159] However, certain events over the past few years point towards a different direction. For example, in 2003 several JMB members were apprehended by the Bangladeshi police with uranium. Police and sources at Bangladesh's Atomic Energy Commission later remarked that they possessed enough uranium to manufacture a dirty bomb.[160] To this day, it is not clearly established why those JMB terrorists were carrying such fissile material and it is still unknown whether they were planning an operation in Bangladesh or acting as couriers for one of their regional partners. Whatever the mission may have been, the consequences of its success would have been cataclysmic.

Second, as briefly mentioned earlier, JMB carried out a near simultaneous terrorist attack on August 17, 2005, when it detonated a total of 463 bombs over a span of 50 minutes in 63 out of 64 district towns in Bangladesh.[161] This was by no means a simple feat as an operation of that nature required superb organization, planning, and coordination to achieve the desired results. Furthermore, each attack site was also left with a leaflet carrying the key messages of the group. The motivations may have been local, but it is unlikely that without support of either a tactical or logistical nature from an international partner, such an operation could have been mounted.

Third, there is now an elaborate structure of financing that is used by Bangladeshi terror groups. A recent study undertaken by the Center for Strategic and International Studies (CSIS) has shown that both HUJI-B and JMB extensively use the large Bangladeshi expatriate population for fund raising and are known to have received funds from Europe and the Middle East. They have also received funds from NGOs in the Middle East.[162] In addition, a HUJI-B terrorist apprehended in 2008 admitted during interrogation that he had undertaken several visits to countries in Southeast Asia. It is also important to note that Maulana Tajuddin, one of the key masterminds of the deadly bomb attack on the Awami League political rally (where the incumbent Bangladeshi Prime Minister was seriously wounded) on August 21, 2004, is currently in South Africa according to various reports.[163] It is believed that South African organizations have been used for raising funds, and, as such, it is clear that the organization has spread far and wide, and its linkages transcend well beyond Bangladesh's immediate vicinity.[164]

The international community must note with caution the potential fissures and divisions that exist within Bangladeshi society. Bangladesh has evolved into a secular society where culture and religion cohabit in the same space without having any contradiction or collision. The terrorist and extremist groups operating in Bangladesh find this to be disdainful, and these groups will continually try to resist the forces in favor of preserving the secular liberal nature of the state. Further, in the aftermath of the mutiny of the BDR in February 2009, it is critically important to examine the kind of fissures that terror groups can create within the security forces of Bangladesh while bearing in mind that HUJI-B also tried to stage a coup in 1995. The attempt was meant to topple the elected government and install an Islamist regime, but the coup was averted due to early intelligence reports.[165] Given the historical, operational, and administrative links that exist between HUJI-P and HUJI-B, this is something that needs to be taken into account. Therefore, there is a requirement to study this dimension of the problem very closely, and it is critical to understand if there has been any Islamist penetration of the security apparatus since it can have catastrophic consequences for the security of Bangladesh and the region.

Links to Groups in India

Many analysts as well as Indian security officials believe that HUJI-B actively works with the banned SIMI, is a component of the Indian Mujahideen as part of its design to expand its support base and to destabilize India, and was possibly involved in the November 2008 Mumbai attacks.[166] HUJI-B poses a very serious threat to Indian security not only because of its links to other transnational terrorist groups that are antagonistic towards New Delhi and have a proven ability to carry out large-scale attacks, but also because many of its cadre do not arouse suspicion as they speak a language (Bangla) and are of an ethnic background (Bengali) that is also prominent in India. This is compounded by the porous nature of the poorly-policed Indo-Bangladesh border and the lack of an extradition treaty between the two countries. As such, future efforts to prevent infiltration will prove most difficult even if sufficient political will is available, something that is debatable.

Like most of India's smaller South Asian neighbors, there is considerable apprehension in Bangladesh regarding New Delhi's ambitions in the subcontinent as well as its perceived interference in Bangladesh's internal affairs. However, at the same time it is not in Bangladesh's interest to have a hostile relationship with its giant neighbor and, as such, any leadership in Dhaka must toe a fine line by maintaining at least a stable relationship with India while not appearing to be too close to New Delhi. Failure to do so risks jeopardizing their domestic as well as international legitimacy and regime security.

Following the most recent election late last year, Sheikh Hasina returned to power. Largely perceived to be pro-India, it has been widely anticipated that her administration will seek to crack down on groups that threaten regional stability, such as JMB and HUJI-B, but also several insurgent groups in India's Northeast that New Delhi believes have taken refuge in

Bangladesh. Much of Hasina's credibility in India will rest upon the extent to which she can effectively reign in these groups, and, given her previous failures, her half-life with the Indians is not incredibly generous. This fact is not lost on her Islamist adversaries who recognize that carrying out attacks in India has a multiplier effect in that it increases the group's profile, enhances its credentials as an international terrorist outfit, and also actively undercuts any potential for improvement in Indo-Bangladesh ties, something that could put a major dent in their activities. It can also provoke irrational responses by India and strengthen hardliners in New Delhi thus creating an environment that is even more conducive to militant activity in both countries. Any attack that HUJI-B or JMB carries out in India has multiple objectives and sophisticated political aims.

Links to groups in Pakistan

HUJI-B was initially an offshoot of HUJI-P, a Pakistan-based Kashmir-centered group that had strong links with the Pakistani security apparatus and, until recently, was the stronger half. Traditionally, HUJI-B has taken much of its training and arms supply from Muzaffarabad in Pakistan-administered Kashmir (PAK) as part of its partnership with HUJI-P, but this has now changed and it has become the role of HUJI-B to maintain relevance by continuing to carry out attacks in Bangladesh and India. Nonetheless, HUJI-B still maintains some of its most critical Pakistani links and interrogations of captured militants have revealed that the group has recently employed trainers from Pakistan-based LeT and JeM. However, as the international spotlight shines brightly on Pakistan, HUJI-B has shifted many of its training and logistical operations into Bangladesh itself, though information sharing still likely continues.[167]

Jalaluddin Haqqani's network has existed in Pakistan since the Soviet era and also extends throughout the Pashtun areas of

Afghanistan and into Kabul. Haqqani is arguably the most credible mujahideen, given his personal history and lack of involvement in Afghanistan's brutal civil war. Further, unlike the Tehrik-i-Taliban Pakistan, the Haqqani network is friendly towards Pakistan, urges other groups to avoid engaging the Pakistani security forces, and focuses all of its resources on Afghanistan. As such, while still being on the receiving end of many American drone strikes, his network has not been the focal point of military operations by the Pakistani Army. Any cooperation between the Haqqani network and HUJI-B could greatly enhance the latter's operational capabilities through training, while also providing HUJI-B with an established infrastructure to raise funds and to hide wanted members. It is of note that over 20 Bangladeshis were arrested while trying to cross the Afghan-Pakistan border in 2008.[168]

Haqqani runs an extensive unregulated network of madrassas near the border with Afghanistan. These schools are often blamed for helping to spawn the Taliban movement in Afghanistan in the 1990s and were known to provide thousands of frontline troops during their advances. Most of the madrassas are still operational and have also been the target of American drone attacks, thus suggesting that they still support insurgents in Afghanistan, domestic and foreign. Bangladesh also has an unregulated network of thousands of private "Qaumi" madrassas that develop their own curriculum and are not required to make their sources of funding known to Dhaka.[169] Any further transfer of radical ideology from overseas into Bangladesh's Qaumi madrassas is extremely dangerous, as this has been a major driver behind groups such as JMB beginning to look beyond Bangladesh in their strategic planning. Further, while Pakistani groups like the TTP and the Tehreek-e-Nafaz-e-Shariat-e-Mohammadi (TNSM) are still somewhat nationalist in nature and locally focused, this is not the case with HUJI-B, a group that is increasingly identifying itself with global terrorism and making less of a distinction between the "far" and "near" enemy. Increased contacts with other radical madrassa networks in South Asia could accelerate this trend. However, it should be noted that, by and large, unregulated Bangladeshi madrassas produce lower-ranking members for HUJI-B and JMB as they do not equip graduates with many practical skills. Nonetheless, these individuals still form the bulk of the membership of these groups and are the ones who are charged with executing attacks and implementing various strategies and directives. HUJI-B and JMB have undoubtedly been watching developments in Pakistan's Malakand Division (which houses Swat) with much interest since, like Sufi Mohammed and the TNSM, one of their main complaints with the Bangladeshi state is over the lack of Sharia law and the slow, inefficient, and corrupt practices that are commonplace in the British-style judiciary. A careful analysis of strategies and tactics used by the TNSM is likely underway, and information exchange cannot be ruled out. HUJI-B and JMB also have latecomer's advantage in that they have been able to witness the successes and failures of previous groups and can avoid many potential pitfalls. As such, expect a deliberate and precise strategy by HUJI-B and JMB that seeks to incorporate many of the lessons learned from other terrorist/ insurgent theaters. Already we are seeing them attempting to employ their own ink blot strategy by building their support base and cadre strength district by district. Further, these groups seek active participation in the legitimate political process: HUJI-B attempted to run in the elections in late 2008 under the Islamic Democratic Party but was denied permission by the Election Commission. Also, JMB has now split and established a mainstream ideological wing that claims to operate separately from the militant outfit and has reconstituted its Shura.[170] All of these developments point to long-term strategic thinking and the intent to systematically intensify their campaigns in the country.

Implications

Just like financial markets, terrorist or insurgent markets influence each other. Successes by terrorist or insurgent organizations in other South Asian theaters will embolden the Bangladeshi groups as well as IM, something that can lead to an increase in recruiting as well as more audacious tactics. Also, as HUJI-B, JMB, and IM are considerably younger and less wellknown than most of their regional counterparts, they will likely attempt to springboard into the limelight through more violent yet innovative methods of attack and subversion. However, this will require guidance from external sources.

Like the rest of the world's most prolific terrorist groups, Bangladesh's organizations have recognized the power of ideas and increasingly sophisticated propaganda videos have begun to appear that are available in multiple forms in order to reach as many potential recruits as possible. In addition, JMB's information operations (IO) are very effective and place great emphasis on leaflets and on immediately explaining the rationale for their actions in a clear and concise manner. For example, JMB explained the lack of massive casualties during their coordinated bomb blasts in 2005 as being the result of an intentional decision to not cause harm to innocents. Instead, they claimed that the bombs were designed to serve as a demonstration of power and a warning to Dhaka. If IM is to become a long-term factor in India, it will also have to develop a more advanced IO capacity.

As JMB is operating in an environment that shares many similarities with India (official secularism, constitutional governance, democratic institutions, etc.), its rationale and justifications for its attacks could provide a useful framework for IM. In addition, the influence of the pan-Islamic Hizbut Tahrir has mushroomed in Bangladesh, while the country still faces a critical shortage of iconic moderate Muslim clerics to counter this development and the increased propagation of radical Islamic ideology. Without an effective counterweight, breaking the recruitment cycle of groups such as HUJI-B and JMB will prove most difficult, if not impossible.

Like the Afghan Taliban in the 1990s, TTP, al-Qaeda, and others, JMB and HUJI-B have creatively blended select Islamic themes and socio-economic issues in a simple, easy-to-digest manner that does not require much critical thinking. This ensures that their ideology is not solely dependent on Islamic arguments, messages that can be countered by qualified religious leaders, thus enhancing its survivability and long-term viability. These groups have also successfully identified their target audience (semi-educated 18-25-year old Bangladeshis with limited employment prospects) and are carrying out an aggressive marketing campaign. HUJI-B and JMB have also seen how causing high civilian casualties and not adhering to local traditions can quickly drain the oxygen out of a movement, something that al-Qaeda in Iraq (AQI) learned the hard way.

Given the close ties between LeT and the HUJI chapters in both Pakistan and Bangladesh that have been forged over the years in Kashmir and elsewhere, coordination of efforts to enhance IM's capabilities is likely. While the world closely analyses Pakistan's every move regarding counterterrorism, Bangladesh is still considered a nonfactor by many. As such, HUJI-B, JMB, and LeT may be able to use Bangladeshi territory to aid IM's efforts to carry out consistent low-tech attacks throughout India, while leaving spectaculars to LeT for the time being. This is not to play down the threat to India originating from Pakistani soil, but several South Asian terrorist groups likely view Bangladesh in the same manner that an investor views an emerging market. Efforts to increase terrorist capacity in India and nearby Bangladesh will be spearheaded by LeT as a component of its strategy to become the most prolific terrorist group in the region.

CONCLUSION

Although LeT was a key component of Islamabad's regional strategy in the past, the organization is growing beyond Pakistan's control and is undertaking its own independent operations. LeT still views Kashmir as a vital issue, but now feels it is a part of a larger Pan-Islamic strategy. Pursuant to this objective, LeT has forged selective partnerships with fellow Pakistani and other regional militant groups, as well as criminal syndicates, whose activities undermine Pakistan's own security, escalate terrorism campaigns throughout South Asia, and increase the risk of an inadvertent war between India and Pakistan. One such group is al-Qaeda, an organization whose presence on Pakistani soil Islamabad has promised to eradicate. LeT is also believed to have been involved in attempts on the lives of several Pakistani leaders, including General Musharraf, and the recent attacks in Mumbai. As such, it appears that LeT leaders no longer feel that they are accountable to their former patron as a whole, but rather to themselves and a select few officers in ISI and the Pakistani military (current and/or retired). However, if support for LeT from the Pakistani intelligence and military establishment continues unabated, LeT will become a multinational organization that determines its own agenda as it will have a wide range of sponsors and sources of funding, and will have fighters and other vital resources spread throughout several regions. This clearly defies the logic, used by several state sponsors of terrorism, that irregulars can be sustainably used in an asymmetric fashion to achieve limited objectives against a conventionally superior adversary, and that such groups will not eventually deviate from the process of not escalating tensions past a certain point. This throws into doubt claims that ties between groups like Hizballah and Tehran/Damascus are a permanent reality and are not vulnerable to fractionalization.

LeT has not had problems in recruitment, as many madrassas in Pakistan remain unsupervised and do not equip graduates with practical skills. Further, communal tension within India has allowed LeT to develop a working relationship with SIMI and to establish IM, assist its operations, and guide its development and strategic planning. In addition, these tensions have made it possible for LeT to recruit within India, thus providing it with ideal operatives that speak without foreign accents, are highly familiar with their surroundings, and have an extensive network of local contacts. Equally troubling is the fact that LeT has upgraded its activities and has begun to operate throughout India and will likely target transportation and economic infrastructure and the political establishment as opposed to Indian security forces exclusively. It has also adopted new methods of destabilization such as recruiting from India's troubled Northeast and smuggling militants into India by sea, a serious infringement on India's sovereignty.

Despite being a proscribed outfit, LeT still enjoys funding from ISI and through donations from a wide range of domestic and overseas sympathizers, including Indian Muslims. Further, after capitalizing on the 2005 earthquake, LeT has been able to reestablish some of its fund-raising activities within Pakistan. On top of this, LeT now raises funds on the internet and has become market-savvy while making legitimate investments in a range of sectors. LeT is also very likely involved in trafficking Afghan heroin, an extremely highyielding venture given the low overhead costs and high domestic and overseas demand. All of this has resulted in a diversification of LeT's financial pipeline, thus reducing the possibility of it being held hostage to a particular party, decreasing its vulnerability to a decapitating strike, and ensuring its continued existence even if it is abandoned by Islamabad entirely.India will continue to face a serious threat from Pakistan-based terrorist groups for the foreseeable future. However, India lacks military options that have strategic-level effects without a significant risk of a military response by Pakistan, and neither Indian nor US policy is likely to be able to reduce the terrorist threat substantially in the short to medium term. Due to this, other Indian extremists will inevitably find inspiration and instruction from the November 2008 Mumbai attacks. Local radicalization is a major goal of the terrorists, and this will remain a major social and political challenge for India.[171] Although LeT spectaculars grab international attention, and inspire others, their impacts on India and Mumbai in particular are not usually long-lasting, thus rendering LeT unable to translate short-term tactical victories into long-term strategic gains while operating on its own from Pakistan. Due to this, LeT and others will rely more heavily on IM to increase its membership and to engage in low-tech terrorism campaigns throughout India if it expects to succeed in undermining the Indian economy, disturbing communal relations, and dashing any hopes of improving ties between India and Pakistan.

Although LeT and groups like HUJI-B have high hopes for IM, the group remains relatively primitive in terms of operational capacity and information operations. LeT's rise to prominence has largely followed a more sophisticated understanding of politics and strategic thought, thus causing the group to come to view violence as a tool rather than an end in itself. IM's urban terrorism currently appears to be reactive and driven by anger rather than by more complex strategic objectives, something that LeT undoubtedly seeks to change. At present, IM's attacks do not require a safe haven or training in Pakistan as they are relatively simple, but if the group intends to evolve, then the role of both Pakistan and Bangladesh will become more prominent. However, although LeT would like to see a much more advanced IM, it will still seek to claim the title of South Asia's most effective terrorist group. If this is to occur, LeT will continue to plan major Mumbai-style operations in India while also scaling up attacks in J&K so as to maintain legitimacy.

Since many of LeT's cadre are Pakistani and IM is still a somewhat disjointed organization, D-Company's logistical network will be critical, especially in major urban centers such as Mumbai. This network can be utilized for recruiting, smuggling weapons and militants in and out of India, and providing pre- and post-operation services like surveillance, reconnaissance, and assisting terrorists in moving through India undetected. Without D-Company's vast cross-border network, LeT is unlikely to be able to achieve its objectives in India and the growth of IM will be inhibited, thus limiting it to inconsistent low tech terrorism which has few lasting effects despite the loss of human life and damage to property. Though investigations are still ongoing and the full story may never be available, as is the case with the 1993 Mumbai (Bombay) blasts, any revelation of D-Company involvement in the 2008 Mumbai attacks should not surprise analysts.

India faces a considerable security challenge from Bangladesh with two major terrorist groups that have ties to LeT and other groups in Pakistan and are increasing their capabilities alongside their ambitions and political awareness while the country has been neglected by international counterterrorism efforts. The bomb blasts in Assam and the

BDR mutiny serve as a startling preview of what is to come if current trends are not reversed. Given the porous nature of the Indo-Bangladeshi border and the shared ethnicity between the two countries, knock-on effects in India and on IM's capabilities would be nearly unavoidable. Further, in the event that Pakistan actually engages in a meaningful crackdown on terrorist groups operating from its territory, Bangladesh would become IM's most viable option for strategic guidance and material support.

No group from Pakistan, Bangladesh, or elsewhere could make headway in India unless conditions in select areas were conducive to such activity. Without the Indian component, these groups would remain confined to carrying out occasional large-scale attacks that do not result in political gains, and the IM project could not be successful. This fact is something that New Delhi must continuously emphasize to its civilian population as opposed to focusing a disproportionate amount of attention on foreign groups. As long as the Indian media and political leadership continue to point the finger exclusively towards external forces, many in the security bodies and the general public will look overseas along with them. If a new counterterrorism body is formed under these misconceptions, there is little to suggest that it will be any more effective than its predecessors. In addition, New Delhi's approach could alienate its regional neighbors, thus unnecessarily undermining any potential for stronger inter-state cooperation. Until New Delhi faces up to this, it is unlikely that it will be able to implement a functioning counterterrorism strategy and these attacks will tragically continue. This will prove most detrimental to India's internal stability, business climate, and the faith of its people in the nation's political leadership and security forces, and could drag South Asia's nuclear-armed rivals into a war.

ENDNOTES

1. B. Raman, "Lashkar-e-Toiba: Spreading the Jehad," The Hindu Business Line, January 5, 2001, available from *www.hinduonnet.com/businessline/2001/01/05/stories/040555ra.htm*.
2. Saeed Shafqat, "From Official Islam to Islamism: The Rise of Dawat-ul-Irshad and Lashkar-e-Taiba," in *Pakistan—Nationalism without a Nation?* C. Jaffrelot, ed., New Delhi, India: Manohar Publishers and Distributors, 2002, pp. 131-149.
3. Raman, "Lashkar-e-Toiba: Spreading the Jehad," 2001.
4. "Profile: Lashkar-e-Toiba," BBC News, March 17, 2006, available from *news.bbc.co.uk/1/hi/world/south_asia/3181925.stm*.
5. Wilson John, "Lashkar-e-Toiba: New Threats Posed by an Old Organization," *Terrorism Monitor*, Vol. 3, Issue 4, February 24, 2005.
6. The primary objective of a *fidayeen* mission is to inflict as many human casualties as possible. Most often, militants attack a target until they themselves are killed. However, unlike suicide bombings, there is a small chance of survival, although it is minimal.
7. "Profile: Lashkar-e-Toiba."
8. "Lashkar-e-Toiba," BBC News, November 25, 2002, available from *news.bbc.co.uk/1/hi/world/south_asia/2510613.stm*; John, 2005.
9. "Lashkar-e-Toiba—'Army of the Pure'," South Asia Terror Portal, 2001, available from *www.satp.org/satporgtp/countries/india/ states/jandk/terrorist_outfits/lashkar_e_toiba.htm*.
10. "ISI Hand in 7/11 Mumbai Blasts, Say Police," *The Hindu*, October 1, 2006, available from *www.hindu.com/2006/10/01/stories/2006100113440100.htm*; Kanchan Lakshman, "The ISI Exposed," *South Asia Intelligence Review*, Vol. 5, No. 12, October 2, 2006.
11. Steven Aftergood, "Lashkar-e-Taiba (Army of the Righteous)," Washington, DC: Federation of American Scientists, May 21, 2004, available from *www.fas.org/irp/world/para/lakshar. htm*.

12. Interview with Bukhari Syed Adnan Ali Shah, International Centre for Political Violence and Terrorism Research, Singapore, March 14, 2008.
13. "Lashkar-e-Toiba" BBC News, 2002.
14. "Profile: Lashkar-e-Toiba"; Samina Yasmeen, "Pakistan's Kashmir Policy: Voices of Moderation?" *Contemporary South Asia*, Vol. 12, No. 2, June 2003. Jama'at ud Dawa has also now been proscribed following the November 2008 Mumbai attacks.
15. Sanjay Jha, "Delhi Blasts, Terror Networks, and India's Internal Security," *Strategic Analysis*, Vol. 29, No. 4, 2005.
16. Tim McGirk, "Lay Down Your Guns," *Time Magazine*, May 12, 2003, available from *www.time.com/time/magazine/ article/ 0,9171,451022,00.html.*
17. M. Khan, "Pakistani Militant's Fluctuating Fate," BBC News, October 24, 2006, available from *news.bbc.co.uk/1/hi/world/ south_asia/6067694.stm.*
18. Interview with Bukhari Syed Adnan Ali Shah.
19. John, "Lashkar-e-Toiba: New Threats Posed by an Old Organization," 2005.
20. M. L. Kak, "ISI Plan to Restructure UJC," *The Tribune*, February 1, 2003, available from *www.tribuneindia. com/2003/20030201/ jandk.htm#1.*
21. Sanjay Jha.
22. "Lashkar-e-Toiba," BBC News, 2002
23. Raman, "Lashkar-e-Toiba, Spreading the Jehad," 2001.
24. K. Sreedhar and Sudhir Manish, "Jihadis in Jammu and Kashmir—A Portrait Gallery," New Delhi, India: Sage Publications, 2003.
25. Both quotes from B. Raman, "The Lashkar-e-Toiba (LeT)," South Asia Analysis Group, Paper No. 374, 2001, pp. 3-4.
26. "Lashkar-e-Toiba- 'Army of the Pure'," 2001. Noor Ismail, "The Role of Kinship in Indonesia's Jemmah Islamiya," *Terrorism Monitor*, Vol. 4, Issue 11, June 2, 2006.
27. "Lashkar-e-Toiba-'Army of the Pure,'" 2001.

28. Raman, "LeT Issues Fatwa to Kill the Pope," *International Terrorism Monitor*, Paper No. 133, South Asia Analysis Group, 2006.
29. Steven Aftergood.
30. Sati Sahni, "Kashmir Underground," New Delhi, India: Har-Anand Publications Pvt. Ltd., 1999.
31. Sreedhar and Manish.
32. David Hardaker, "The World Today—Background to Lashkar-e-Toiba," ABC Online, November 5, 2003, available from *www.abc.net.au/worldtoday/content/2003/s982752.html.*
33. Raman, "The Lashkar-e-Toiba (LeT)," 2001.
34. Ashima Kaul, "The Proliferation of Small Arms in J&K," *Control Arms India Update*, Vol. 1, No. 2, 2005.
35. Hardaker.
36. "ISI Agent Held in Hyderabad," *The Hindu*, April 2, 2007, available from *www.thehindu.com/2007/04/02/stories/2007040217231100.htm.*
37. Thangjam Singh, "Could Pune be a Future Terrorist Target?" *IDSA Strategic Comments*, August 17, 2006, New Delhi, India: Institute for Defence Studies and Analyses.
38. Ved Marwah, "India's Internal Security Challenges," *Strategic Analysis*, Vol. 27, No. 4, 2003.
39. Praveen Swami and Mohammed Shehzad, "Lashkar Raising Islamist Brigades for Iraq," *The Hindu*, June 13, 2004, available from *www.hindu.com/2004/06/13/stories/2004061306050100.htm.*
40. "Profile: Lashkar-e-Toiba"; "Lashkar-e-Toiba," BBC News, 2002.
41. Sreedhar and Manish.
42. Nigel Brew, "Lashkar-e-Taiba (LeT) and the Threat to Australia," Research Note, No. 36, February 16, 2004, Information Analysis and Advice for the Parliament, Department of Parliamentary Services, Canberra, Australia.
43. "Lashkar-e-Toiba-'Army of the Pure'," 2001.
44. Ghulam Hasnain, "Inside Jihad," *Time Asia*, Vol. 157, No. 5, February 5, 2001; Khan, 2006.

45. John, "Lashkar-e-Toiba: New Threats Posed by an Old Organization," 2005. His methodology for establishing this figure is unknown and should not be taken as an indisputable fact.
46. Jessica Stern, "Pakistan's Jihad Culture," *Foreign Affairs*, November/December 2000.
47. Sreedhar and Manish.
48. Interview with Bukhari Syed Adnan Ali Shah; Interview with Mahsud Saif Ullah Khan, International Centre for Political Violence and Terrorism Research, Singapore, March 14, 2008.
49. "LeT Recruiting Afghan Refugees to Support Taliban in Afghanistan," *Terrorism Focus*, Vol. 3, Issue 39, October 10, 2006.
50. Daan Van Der Schriek, "Nuristan: Insurgent Hideout in Afghanistan," *Terrorism Monitor*, Vol. 3, Issue 10, May 19, 2005.
51. Raman, "LeT Issues Fatwa to Kill the Pope"; John, "Lashkor-e-Toiba: New Threats Posed by an Old Organization," 2005.
52. John, "Lashkar-e-Toiba: New Threats Posed by an Old Organization," 2005.
53. Sreedhar and Manish.
54. "Lashkar-e-Toiba," BBC News, 2002.
55. "Lashkar Militant Admits Killing Sikhs in Chittisinghpura," *Rediff*, December 31, 2000, p. 1, available from *www.Rediff. com/news/2000/dec/31sikh.htm.*
56. "Who are the Kashmir Militants?" BBC News, February 19, 2003, available from *news.bbc.co.uk/1/low/world/south_asia/1719612. stm.*
57. "Profile: Lashkar-e-Toiba." 58. *Ibid.*
59. "Pakistan Freezes Militant Funds," BBC News, December 24, 2001, available from *news.bbc.co.uk/1/hi/world/south_ asia/1726813.stm.*
60. Aftergood.
61. "Lashkar-e-Toiba," BBC News, 2002.
62. Aftergood.
63. Brew.

64. "Profile: Lashkar-e-Toiba."
65. "Lashkar-e-Toiba-'Army of the Pure,'" 2001.
66. "Pakistan's 'Role in Mumbai Attacks'," BBC News, September 30, 2006, available from *news.bbc.co.uk/1/hi/world/south_asia/5394686.stm*.
67. Zubair Ahmed, "Mumbai Marks a Grim Anniversary," BBC News, July 10, 2007, available from *news.bbc.co.uk/1/hi/world/south_asia/6288916.stm*.
68. "LeT Threat to Dalai Lama," *Daily Excelsior*, April 2, 2007, available from *www.dailyexcelsior.com/web1/07apr02/news.htm#9*.
69. "Anatomy of Evil," *The Indian Express*, July 11, 2007, available from *www.indianexpress.com/story/204473.html*.
70. *Ibid.*
71. *Ibid.*
72. *Ibid.*
73. "Man Arrested in Nepal with Fake Indian Currency," *Dawn*, August 1, 2007, available from *www.dawn.com/2007/08/01/top21.htm*.
74. "LeT Suspect Nabbed," *The Times of India*, July 13, 2007, available from *timesofindia.indiatimes.com/cities/LeT_suspect_nabbed/ articleshow/2199336.cms*.
75. M. Singh, "Growing Fundamentalism in the Northeast," *IDSA Strategic Comments*, February 19, 2007, New Delhi, India: Institute for Defence Studies and Analyses.
76. Anil Bhat, "From Inverted Crescent to Full Moon and Jihadi Pincer," *The Statesman*, June 26, 2007, available from *thestatesman. co.in page.arcview.php?clid=14andid=188731 andusrsess=1*.
77. M. Singh, " Growing Fundamentalism in the Northeast," 2007.
78. Thangjam Singh, "The LeT Menace in Delhi," *IDSA Strategic Comments*, May 11, 2007, New Delhi, India: Institute for Defence Studies and Analyses.
79. Aftergood.
80. Sreedhar and Manish.
81. Aftergood.

82. "Profile: Lashkar-e-Toiba.".
83. Khan.
84. Praveen Swami, "Quake Came as a Boon for Lashkar Leadership," *The Hindu*, November 17, 2005, available from *www.thehindu.com/2005/11/17/stories/2005111705951200.htm*.
85. Joshua Partlow and Kamran Khan, "Charity Funds Said to Provide Clues to Alleged Terrorist Plot," *Washington Post*, August 15, 2006.
86. "Meet the Lashkar-e-Tayiba's Fundraiser," *Rediff*, July 28, 2006, available from *www.Rediff.com///news/2006/jul/28lashkar.htm*.
87. Stern.
88. Brew.
89. Mohammad Shehzad, "Banned LeT Collects Millions in Charity Hides," *South Asia Tribune*, Issue 35, March 23-29, 2003.
90. Karen Tandy, "Afghanistan: Law Enforcement Interdiction Efforts in Transshipment Countries to Stem the Flow of Heroin," Testimony before the Subcommittee on Criminal Justice, Drug Policy and Human Resources, U.S. House of Representatives, Washington DC, February 26, 2004, available from *www.usdoj.gov/dea/pubs/cngrtest/ct022604.htm*; "70% Afghan Narcotics Move through Pakistan," *Daily Times*, March 22, 2005, available from *www.dailytimes.com.pk/default.asp?page=story_22-3-2005_pg7_35*.
91. Rollie Lal, "South Asian Organized Crime and Terrorist Networks," *Orbis*, Vol. 49, Issue 2, Spring 2005.
92. *Ibid.*
93. Malik Mustafa, "Proliferation of Small Arms and Light Weapons: Case Study - South Asia," *Strategic Studies*, Vol. XXV, No. 2, Summer 2005.
94. "A Godfather's Lethal Mix of Business and Politics," *U.S. News and World Report*, November 27, 2005; available from *www.usnews.com/usnews/news/articles/051205/5terror.b.htm*.
95. Praveen Swami, "Flawed justice," *Frontline*, Vol. 23, Issue 19, September 23-October 06, 2006.

96. Praveen Swami, "Harnessing hate," *Frontline*, Vol. 23, Issue 15, July 29-August 11, 2006.

97. Praveen Swami, "Nairobi Arrest Points to Deepening Lashkar-Dawood Links," *The Hindu*, July 22, 2006, available from *www.hindu.com/2006/07/22/stories/2006072225171800.htm.*

98. Paul Watson and Siddhartha Barua, "Camps Thrive in Pakistan, India Charges," *Los Angeles Times*, January 11, 2002.

99. Bisheshwar Mishra, "ISI, Dawood Help LeT Set a Global Network," *The Times of India*, July 2, 2003, p. 1, available from *timesofindia.indiatimes.com/articleshow/56386.cms.*

100. Mishra.

101. Amir Mir, "Catch Me if You Can," *Mid Day*, November 9, 2003.

102. Daniel Byman, *et al.*, "Trends in Outside Support for Insurgent Movements" Santa Monica, CA: RAND Corporation, 2001.

103. *Ibid.*

104. Daniel Byman, "The Changing Nature of State Sponsorship of Terrorism," Analysis Paper, No. 16, May 2008, Washington, DC: Saban Center for Middle East Policy, Brookings Institute, pp. 25-26.

105. *Ibid.*

106. Daniel Byman, "Passive Support of Terrorism," MIT Security Studies Seminar, October 6, 2004, p. 1.

107. Ahmed Rashid, "How to succeed and fail in FATA," *Daily Times*, February 5, 2008, available from *www.dailytimes.com.pk.*

108. Byman, "Passive Support of Terrorism."

109. Emile El-Hokayem, "Hizballah and Syria: Outgrowing the Proxy Relationship," *The Washington Quarterly*, Spring 2007, p. 36.

110. Jonathan Pike, "Directorate for Inter-Services Intelligence [ISI]," Washington, DC: Federation of American Scientists, 2002, available from *www.fas.org/irp/world/pakistan/isi/*

111. Rahul Bedi, "Vital Intelligence on the Taliban May Rest with its Prime Sponsor—Pakistan's ISI," Jane's Information Group, October 1, 2001, available from *www.janes.com/security/international_security/news/misc/janes011001_1_n.shtml.*

112. Selig Harrison, "Stop Building Up Pakistani Military Capacities Against India," *The International Herald Tribune*, December 20, 2001, available from *www.iht.com/articles/2001/12/20/edsig_ed3_.php*.

113. "Kashmir: An Insurgency Wedged Between Two Nuclear Powers," *Jane's Intelligence Backgrounder*, 2001.

114. Interview with Pakistani diplomat, February 13, 2009, Singapore.

115. Both quotes from Roger Hardy, "Pakistan's 'Culture of Jihad'," BBC News, August 5, 2002, p. 4, available from *news.bbc.co.uk/1/hi/in_depth/world/2002/islamic_world/2173818.stm*.

116. Kashmir.

117. Stern; Hardaker.

118. Khan.

119. Michel Chossudovsky, "The Foiled UK Terror Plot and the 'Pakistani Connection'," *Global Research*, August 14, 2006.

120. Singh, "The LeT Menace in Delhi."

121. Raman, "The Lashkar-e-Toiba (LeT)," 2001.

122. Phillip Smucker, "Al-Qaeda Thriving in Pakistani Kashmir," *Christian Science Monitor*, July 2, 2002, available from *www.csmonitor.com/2002/0702/p01s02-wosc.html*; Swami and Shehzad.

123. Amir Mir, "The Jihad Lives On," *Asia Times*, March 11, 2005, available from *www.atimes.com/atimes/South_Asia/GC11Df07.html*.

124. Ryan Clarke, "The Indigenization of Terrorism in India," RSIS Commentary, S. Rajaratnam School of International Studies, Singapore, December 26, 2008.

125. Bruce Riedel, "Terrorism in India and the Global Jihad," Washington, DC: Brookings Institute, November 30, 2008.

126. Brian Jenkins, "Terrorists Can Think Strategically— Lessons Learned from the Mumbai Attacks," Testimony presented before the Senate Homeland Security and Governmental Affairs Committee, January, 28, 2009.

127. Angel Rabasa, *et al.*, "The Lessons of Mumbai," Occasional Paper, Washington, DC: RAND Corporation, 2009.

128. Jenkins.
129. Rabasa *et al.*
130. *Ibid.*
131. *Ibid.*
132. Interview with Indian security analyst, April 16, 2009.
133. Rabasa, *et al.*
134. Jenkins.
135. Rabasa *et al.*
136. "Lawyer Named for Mumbai Suspect," BBC News, March 30, 2009, available from *www.bbc.co.uk*.
137. Rabasa, *et al.*
138. *Ibid.*
139. *Ibid.*
140. Michael Scheuer, "Islamabad Rides a Terror Tiger," *Asia Times*, September 20, 2008, available from *www.atimes.com*.
141. Praveen Swami, "India's Elections and the Islamist Terror Threat," Asian Conflict Reports, Issue 4, April 2009.
142. *Ibid.*
143. Scheuer.
144. *Ibid.*
145. Animesh Roul, "Lashkar-e-Taiba Resumes Operations Against Indian Forces in Jammu and Kashmir," *Terrorism Monitor*, Vol. VII, Issue 8, April 3, 2009.
146. *Ibid.*
147. Syed Saleem Shazad, "The Rise and Rise of the Neo- Taliban," *Asia Times*, April 2, 2009, available from *www.atimes. com*.
148. *Ibid.*
149. Syed Saleem Shahzad, "Pakistan Braces for More Attacks," *Asia Times*, April 1, 2009.
150. *Ibid.*
151. Farhana Ali and Mohammed Shehzad, "Lashkar-i- Tayyiba Remains Committed to Jihad," *CTC Sentinel*, Vol. 2, Issue 3, March 2009.

152. *Ibid.*

153. Siddharth Srivastava, "India Faces Terror from Another Front," *Asia Times*, November 13, 2008, available from *www.atimes.com*.

154. *Ibid.*

155. Khaled Iqbal Chowdhury, "BDR Mutiny and Its Security Implications," Dhaka: Bangladesh Institute of Peace and Security Studies (BIPSS) Special Report, March 2009.

156. Wilson John, "The Bengali Taleban," *Terrorism Monitor*, Vol. 6, Issue 10, May 15, 2008.

157. Conclusions drawn by the author after extensively viewing propaganda videos produced by Bangladeshi terrorist groups.

158. *Ibid.*

159. For example, M. Aynul Islam, "Let's Consider Micro- Actors in Anti-Terrorism Exercise," *Daily Star*, February 14, 2009.

160. Josh Kurlantzick and Anirudh Suri, "Bangladesh: State in Decline," Washington, DC: Carnegie Endowment for International Peace, January 15, 2007, available from *www.carnegieendowment.* org/publications/index.cfm?fa=viewandid=18968andprog=zgpandpr *oj=zsa*; Interview with Bangladeshi security analyst, August 25, 2009.

161. "Bombs Explode Across Bangladesh," BBC, August 17, 2005.

162. Anupam Ray, "Islamic Radical Ideologies and South Asian Security: The Case of Bangladesh," Washington, DC: Center for Strategic and International Studies, October 27, 208, available from *www.csis.org/component/option,com_csis_pubs/task,view/id,5103/*.

163. "Interpol Issued Red Notice for Grenade Supplier," *Daily Star*, August 21, 2008.

164. Interview with Bangladeshi security analyst, August 25, 2009.

165. Owen Bennet Jones, "Pakistan: The Eye of The Storm," New Haven, CT: Yale University Press, 2003; Interview with Bangladeshi security analyst, August 25, 2009.

166. Ryan Clarke, "The Indigenization of Terrorism in India," *RSIS Commentary*, Singapore: S. Rajaratnam School of International Studies, December 26, 2008.

167. Interviews with Bangladeshi and Pakistani security analysts, August 26, 2009.

168. *Ibid.*

169. Interview with Bangladeshi security analyst, August 24, 2009.

170. *Ibid.*

171. Rabasa *et al.*

REFERENCES

"A Godfather's Lethal Mix of Business and Politics," U.S. News and World Report, November 27, 2005.

www.usnews.com/usnews/news/articles/*051205/5terror.b.htm.*

Aftergood, Steven, "Lashkar-e-Taiba (Army of the Righteous)," Washington, DC: Federation of American Scientists, May 21, 2004. *www.fas.org/irp/*world/para/lakshar.htm.

Ahmed, Zubair, "Mumbai Marks a Grim Anniversary," BBC News, July 10, 2007. *news.bbc.co.uk/1/hi/world/ south_asia/6288916.stm.*

Ali, Farhana and Shehzad, Mohammed, "Lashkari-Tayyiba Remains Committed to Jihad," *CTC Sentinel*, Vol. 2, Issue 3, March 2009.

"Anatomy of Evil," *The Indian Express*, July 11, 2007. *www.indianexpress.com/story/204473.html.*

Bedi, Rahul, "Vital Intelligence on the Taliban May Rest with Its Prime Sponsor—Pakistan's ISI," Jane's Information Group, October 1, 2001. *www.*janes.com/security/international_security/news/misc/ *janes011001_1_n.shtml.*

Bhat, Anil, "From Inverted Crescent to Full Moon & Jihadi Pincer," *The Statesman*, June 26, 2007. thestatesman.co.in/ page.arcview.php?clid=14&id=188 *31&usrsess=1.*

"Bombs Explode Across Bangladesh," BBC News,August 17, 2005. *www.bbc.co.uk.*

Brew, Nigel, "Lashkar-e-Taiba (LeT) and the Threat to Australia," Research Note, No. 36, February 16, 2004. Information Analysis and Advice for the Parliament, Department of Parliamentary Services, Canberra.

Burr, J.Millar and O'Collins, Robert, "Alms for Jihad: Charity and Terrorism in the Islamic World," Cambridge, UK: Cambridge University Press, 2006.

Byman, Daniel, "The Changing Nature of State Sponsorship of Terrorism," Analysis Paper, No. 16, May 2008. Washington, DC: Brookings Institute, Saban Center for Middle East Policy, pp. 25-26.

____________, "Passive Support of Terrorism," MIT Security Studies Seminar, October 6, 2004, p. 1.

Byman, Daniel *et al.*, "Trends in Outside Support for Insurgent Movements," RAND Corporation, 2001.

Chossudovsky, Michel, "The Foiled UK Terror Plot and the 'Pakistani Connection'," *Global Research*, August 14, 2006.

Chowdhury, Khaled Iqbal, "BDR Mutiny and Its Security Implications," Bangladesh Institute of Peace and Security Studies (BIPSS) Special Report, Dhaka, March 2009.

Clarke, Ryan, "The Indigenization of Terrorism in India," RSIS Commentary, Singapore: S. Rajaratnam School of International Studies, December 26, 2008.

Deyer, Simon, "Concern Mounts Over Bangladesh Madrassas after Bombs," *Daily Times*, September 29, 2005. *www.dailytimes.com.pk.*

El-Hokayem, Emile, "Hizballah and Syria: Outgrowing the Proxy Relationship," *The Washington Quarterly*, Spring 2007, p. 36.

Hardaker, David, "The World Today—Background to Lashkar-e-Toiba," *ABC Online*, November 5, 2003. www.abc.net.au/worldtoday/content/2003/s982752.html.

Hardy, Roger, "Pakistan's 'Culture of Jihad'," BBC News, August 5, 2002. *news.bbc.co.uk/1/hi/in_depth/world/2002/islamic_world/2173818.stm.*

Harrison, Selig, "Stop Building Up Pakistani Military Capacities Against India," *The International Herald Tribune*, December 20, 2001. *www.iht.com/articles/2001/12/20/edsig_ed3_.php.*

Hasnain, Ghulam, "Inside Jihad," *Time Asia*, Vol. 157,

No. 5, February 5, 2001.

Islam, M. Aynul, "Lets Consider Micro-Actors in Anti- Terrorism Exercise," *Daily Star*, February 14, 2009.

"Interpol Issued Red Notice for Grenade Supplier," *Daily Star*, August 21, 2008.

"ISI Agent held in Hyderabad," *The Hindu*, April 2, 2007.

www.thehindu.com/2007/04/02/stories/2007040217231100.htm.

"ISI hand in 7/11 Mumbai Blasts, Say Police," *The Hindu*, October 1, 2006. *www.hindu.com/2006/10/01/stories/2006100113440100.htm.*

Ismail, Noor, "The Role of Kinship in Indonesia's Jemmah Islamiya," *Terrorism Monitor*, Vol. 4, Issue 11, June 2, 2006.

Jenkins, Brian, "Terrorists Can Think Strategically—Lessons Learned from the Mumbai Attacks,"Testimony presented before the Senate Homeland Security and Governmental Affairs Committee, January, 28, 2009.

Jha, Sanjay, "Delhi Blasts, Terror Networks, and India's Internal Security," *Strategic Analysis*, Vol. 29, No. 4, 2005.

John, Wilson, "Lashkar-e-Toiba: New Threats Posed by an Old Organization," *Terrorism Monitor*, Vol. 3, Issue 4, February 24, 2005.

____________, "The Bengali Taleban," *Terrorism Monitor,* Vol. 6, Issue 10, May 15, 2008.

Jones, Owen Bennet, "Pakistan: The Eye of The Storm," New Haven, CT: Yale University Press, 2003.

Kak, M.L., "ISI plan to restructure UJC," *The Tribune*, February 1, 2003. *www.tribuneindia.com/2003/20030201/j&k.htm#1.*

"Kashmir: An Insurgency Wedged Between Two Nuclear Powers," *Jane's Intelligence Backgrounder*, 2001.

Kaul, Ashima, "The Proliferation of Small Arms in J&K," *Control Arms India Update*, Vol. 1, No. 2, 2005.

Khan, M., "Pakistani Militant's Fluctuating Fate," BBC News, October 24, 2006. *news.bbc.co.uk/1/hi/world/ south_asia/6067694.stm.*

Kumar, Anand, "Bangladesh: Islamists Attempt to Regroup," Paper 2351, South Asia Analysis Group, August 30, 2007, New Delhi. *www.southasiaanalysis. org/default.asp.*

Kurlantzick, Josh and Suri, Anirudh, "Bangladesh: State in Decline," Washington, DC: Carnegie Endowment for International Peace, January 15, 2007. *www.carnegieendowment.org/publicationsindex.cfm?fa=view&id=18968&prog=zgp&proj=zsa.*

Lakshman, Kanchan, "The ISI Exposed," *South Asia Intelligence Review*, Vol. 5, No. 12, October 2, 2006.

Lal, Rollie, "South Asian Organized Crime and Terrorist Networks," *Orbis*, Vol. 49, Issue 2, Spring 2005.

"Lashkar-e-Toiba—'Army of the Pure'," South Asia Terror Portal, 2001. *www.satp.org/satporgtp/countries/india/states/jandk/terrorist_outfits/lashkar_e_toiba.htm.*

"Lashkar-e-Toiba," BBC News, November 25, 2002. *news.bbc.co.uk/1/hi/world/south_asia/2510613.stm.*

"Lashkar Militant Admits Killing Sikhs in Chittisinghpura," *Rediff,* December 31, 2000. *www. rediff.com/news/2000/dec/31sikh.htm.*

"Lawyer Named for Mumbai Suspect," BBC News,March 30, 2009. *www.bbc.co.uk.*

"LeT Recruiting Afghan Refugees to Support Taliban in Afghanistan," *Terrorism Focus*, Vol. 3, Issue 39, October 10, 2006.

"LeT Suspect Nabbed," *The Times of India*, July 13, 2007. *timesofindia.indiatimes.com/cities/LeT_suspect_nabbed/articleshow/2199336.cms.*

"LeT Threat to Dalai Lama," *Daily Excelsior*, April 2, 2007. *www.dailyexcelsior.com/web1/07apr02/news. htm#9.*

"Man Arrested in Nepal with Fake Indian Currency," *Dawn*, August 1, 2007. *www.dawn.com/2007/08/01/top21.htm.*

Marwah, Ved, "India's Internal Security Challenges," *Strategic Analysis*, Vol. 27, No. 4, 2003.

McGirk, Tim, "Lay Down Your Guns," *Time Magazine*, May 12,2003.*www.time.com/time/magazine/article/0,9171,451022,00.html.*

"Meet the Lashkar-e-Tayiba's Fundraiser," *Rediff,* July 28, 2006. *www.rediff.com///news/2006/jul/28lashkar. htm.*

Mir, Amir, "Catch Me If You Can," *Mid Day*, November 9, 2003.

___________, "The Jihad Lives On," *Asia Times*, March 11, 2005. *www.atimes.com/atimes/South_Asia/ GC11Df07.html.*

Mishra, Bisheshwar, "ISI, Dawood Help LeT Set a Global Network," *The Times of India*, July 2, 2003. *timesofindia.indiatimes.com/articleshow/56386.cms.*

Mustafa, Malik, "Proliferation of Small Arms and Light Weapons: Case Study—South Asia," *Strategic Studies*, Vol. XXV, No. 2, Summer 2005.

"Pakistan Freezes Militant Funds," BBC News, December 24, 2001. *news.bbc.co.uk/1/hi/world/south_ asia/1726813.stm.*

"Pakistan's 'Role in Mumbai Attacks'," BBC News, September 30, 2006. *news.bbc.co.uk/1/hi/world/south_asia/5394686.stm.*

Partlow, Joshua, and Khan, Kamran, "Charity Funds Said to Provide Clues to Alleged Terrorist Plot," *Washington Post*, August 15, 2006.

Pike, Jonathan, "Directorate for Inter-Services Intelligence [ISI]," Washington, DC: Federation of American Scientists, 2002. *www.fas.org/ irp/world/ pakistan/isi/.*

"Profile: Lashkar-e-Toiba," BBC News, March 17, 2006. *news.bbc.co.uk/1/hi/world/south_asia/3181925.stm.*

Rabasa, Angel *et al.*, "The Lessons of Mumbai," Occasional Paper, RAND Corporation, Washington DC, 2009.

Raman, B., "Lashkar-e-Toiba: Spreading the Jehad," The Hindu Business Line, January 5, 2001. www.hinduonnet.com/businessline/2001/ 01/05/ *stories/040555ra.htm.*

___________, "The Lashkar-e-Toiba (LeT)," South Asia Analysis Group, Paper No. 374, 2001.

___________, "Taliban: Militant Islam, Oil and Fundamentalism in Central Asia," New Haven, CT: Yale University Press, 2001.

___________, "LeT Issues Fatwa to Kill the Pope," *International Terrorism Monitor*, Paper No. 133, 2006, South Asia Analysis Group.

___________, "How to Succeed and Fail in FATA," *Daily Times*, February 5, 2008. *www.dailytimes.com. pk.*

Ray, Anupam, "Islamic Radical Ideologies and South Asian Security: The Case of Bangladesh," Washington, DC: Center for Strategic and International Studies, October 27, 2008. *www.* csis.org/component/ option,com_csis_pubs/task,view/ *id,5103/.*

Riedel, Bruce, "Terrorism in India and the Global Jihad," Washington, DC: Brookings Institute, November 30, 2008.

Roul, Animesh, "Lashkar-e-Taiba Resumes Operations Against Indian Forces in Jammu and Kashmir," *Terrorism Monitor*, Vol. VII, Issue 8, April 3, 2009.

Sahni, Sati, "Kashmir Underground," New Delhi, India: Har-Anand Publications Pvt. Ltd., 1999.

Scheuer, Michael, "Islamabad Rides a Terror Tiger,"*Asia Times*, September 20, 2008. *www.atimes.com.*

Schriek, Daan Van Der, "Nuristan: Insurgent Hideout in Afghanistan," *Terrorism Monitor*, Vol. 3, Issue 10, May 19, 2005.

"70% Afghan narcotics move through Pakistan," *Daily Times*, March 22, 2005. *www.dailytimes.com.pk/ default.asp?page=story_22-3-2005_pg7_35.*

Shafqat, Saeed, "From Official Islam to Islamism: The Rise of Dawat-ul-Irshad and Lashkar-e-Taiba," in *Pakistan—Nationalism without a Nation?* Jaffrelot, C., ed., New Delhi, India: Manohar Publishers & Distributors, 2002, pp. 131-149.

Shazad, Syed Saleem, "The Rise and Rise of the Neo- Taliban," *Asia Times*, April 2, 2009 (a). *www.atimes.com.*

____________, "Pakistan braces for more attacks," *Asia Times*, April 1, 2009(b).

Shehzad, Mohammad, "Banned LeT Collects Millions in Charity, Hides," *South Asia Tribune*, Issue 35, March 23-29, 2003.

Singh, M., "Growing Fundamentalism in the Northeast," *IDSA Strategic Comments*, February 19, 2007, New Delhi, India: Institute for Defence Studies and Analyses.

Singh, Thangjam, "Could Pune be a Future Terrorist Target?," *IDSA Strategic Comments*, August 17, 2006, New Delhi, India: Institute for Defence Studies and Analyses.

____________, "The LeT Menace in Delhi," *IDSA Strategic Comments*, May 11, 2007(b), New Delhi, India: Institute for Defence Studies and Analyses.

Smucker, Phillip, "Al-Qaeda Thriving in Pakistani Kashmir," *Christian Science Monitor*, July 2, 2002. *www.csmonitor.com/2002/ 0702/p01s02-wosc.html.*

Srivastava, Siddharth, "India Faces Terror from Another Front," *Asia Times*, November 13, 2008. *www.atimes.com.*

Sreedhar, K. and Manish, Sudhir, "Jihadis in Jammu and Kashmir—A Portrait Gallery," New Delhi, India: Sage Publications, 2003.

Stern, Jessica, "Pakistan's Jihad Culture," *Foreign Affairs*, November/December 2000.

Swami, Praveen and Shehzad, Mohammed, "Lashkar Raising Islamist Brigades for Iraq," *The Hindu*, June 13, 2004. *www.hindu.com/2004/06/13/stories/ 200406 1306050100.htm.*

Swami, Praveen, "Flawed justice," *Frontline*, Vol. 23, Issue 19, September 23-October 06, 2006.

___________, "Harnessing hate," *Frontline*, Vol. 23, Issue 15, July 29-August 11, 2006.

___________, "Nairobi Arrest Points to Deepening Lashkar-Dawood Links," *The Hindu*, July 22, 2006. *www.hindu.com/2006/07/22/stories/ 2006072225171800.htm.*

___________, "Quake Came as a Boon for Lashkar Leadership," *The Hindu*, November 17, 2005. *ww.thehindu.com/2005/11/17/stories/ 2005111705951200.htm.*

___________, "India's Elections and the Islamist Terror Threat," Asian Conflict Reports, Issue 4, April 2009.

Tandy, Karen, "Afghanistan: Law Enforcement Interdiction Efforts in Transshipment Countries to Stem the Flow of Heroin," Testimony before the Subcommittee on Criminal Justice, Drug Policy and Human Resources, U.S. House of Representatives, Washington DC, February 26, 2004. *www.usdoj.gov/* dea/pubs/cngrtest/ct022604.htm.

Watson, Paul & Barua, Siddhartha, "Camps Thrive in Pakistan, India Charges," *Los Angeles Times*, January 11, 2002.

"Who are the Kashmir Militants?," BBC News, February 19, 2003. *news.bbc.co.uk/1/low/world/south_ asia/1719612.stm.*

Yasmeen, Samina, "Pakistan's Kashmir Policy: Voices of Moderation?" *Contemporary South Asia*, Vol. 12, No. 2, June 2003.

INDEX